J. EDSON LEONARD

Feather in the Breeze

THE LYONS PRESS
Guilford, Connecticut
An imprint of The Globe Pequot Press

OTHER BOOKS BY THE SAME AUTHOR

Flies

Flyrod Casting

Baitrod Casting

The Essential Fly Tier

Solomon Leonard and His Descendants

The Lyons Press is an imprint of The Globe Pequot Press.

10 9 8 7 6 5 4 3 2 1

Printed in the United States of America

Library of Congress Cataloging-in-Publication Data

Leonard, J. Edson
    Feather in the breeze : tales from a fishing life / J. Edson Leonard.
        p. cm.
    Originally published: Rockville Centre, N.Y. : Freshet Press, 1974.
    ISBN 1-59228-224-5
    1. Fly fishing. 2. Saltwater fly fishing. I. Title

SH456.L44 2004
79.12'4--dc22   2004041796

To Moosey
who understands the ways
of a fly fisherman

ACKNOWLEDGMENT

I wish to thank CBS Publications, a division of Columbia Broadcasting System, Inc., for the privilege of including several features written by the author and appearing in *Field and Stream* Magazine.

Contents

Beginnings

The love for fishing and hunting has been in my genes for centuries. Inescapable and at times overwhelming, it caused me no end of difficulties at school, for I found that solving the mysteries of a river was far more to my liking than the hypotheses of Pythagoras. Even in later years I had to develop an almost monastic sense for controlling it.

One of my early forbears had much to do with it, if genes are as responsible for heredity as science proclaims. And my father, a gentle man indeed, whom I fortunately appreciated long before he waded the river for the last time, was also blessed with an abundance of those genes, as were my grandfather and great grandfather. To them the art of flyrodding was no temporal act. It was always part of the weekly agenda, and I suspect that other considerations were sometimes set aside in favor of it. In the case of my father, when the rigors of business became untenable, Dad simply locked up, got his tackle box and me and drove the short ten miles to the slough of Fishing Creek.

The family legend is that that forbear whom we all blame—but whose name has been conferred on no fewer than five of our succeeding generations—was considered inscrutable for having left the forge of his father's blacksmith shop to hunt "painters," those big cats that caterwauled far into the nights of the Massachusetts forests. The last that was known about him was his departure for the Green Mountains of Vermont, doubtless in pursuit of more and bigger "painters." So the story goes, he left with only his 30-caliber, round-ball, revolving-barrel rifle and a modicum of clothing.

I never followed his footsteps to hunt panthers in New England which were all but gone when I first saw the light of day in California. But I have often wondered what I might have done, if given the same opportunity, the same point in time.

When I was hardly nine, my parents moved to Pennsylvania. "We're going home," Dad said. And remembering the stories he had told me about the deer and bear, the native trout, the black bass and Susquehanna "salmon" of his home state and especially those fantastic yarns about the "painter" hunter, I was beside myself. The first thing I did that night he told me about the moving was to clean the little steel flyrod and brass reel he had given me and to oil them until they shone. "Learn to take care of your tackle," he said. "When you are old enough, you'll have your gun." After every fishing trip I had always cleaned my gear, hoping to prove that one day I would be worthy of the fulfillment of that promise.

The long journey by auto to Pennsylvania was unforgettable. Dad had a Cleveland touring car, a big 6-cylinder machine with wide running boards, two spare tires strapped to the back, and an exhaust cut-out that made the Cleveland throb like a fire engine. For the nearly 3000 miles to Pennsylvania I pestered the man to pull the lever on the cut-out which, on occasion, he would concede to do—particularly on a steep grade when each pulse of that old engine resounded like the blast of a duck gun.

The Cleveland was loaded to the limit, but there was room for my little rod in the shallow space above the back seat, just under the mica window that was the shape of a dog biscuit. The Cleveland needed repairs occasionally, and when it did the first place I would look for was a stream or a pond. And ever the understanding and patient man that he was, Dad always managed to find a place to camp or a tourist cabin not far from some sort of fishing. So it was that as a youngster of not yet nine, I virtually fished my way from coast to coast, experiencing the spaciousness of the United States in the early 1920's.

From the first day we left Los Angeles I chattered about the trout and especially the River Bass I would catch. I asked Dad to tell me over and over again how he caught them with a nightcrawler on a spoonhook. "I'll show you how," he had said. "We'll troll for them." Many nights I fell asleep utterly weary, even for a boy, from the bouncing and twisting over the 200 miles a day that Dad attempted to attain. But seldom did I close my eyes until after I had cast at least a few times for something with fins and scales.

I dreamed of that moment drawing nearer each day, of seeing the great Susquehanna whose very name had become magic. We reached the Susquehanna late at night, however, because Dad wanted to make Scranton before the next day without stopping, and Scranton was still hours away. I was sound asleep, and my mother prevailed upon Dad not to wake me up. So it was not the Susquehanna I first saw when I awakened but the Lackawanna. When I saw its flow, inky black from the coal washing in the collieries, I was horrified and I wept bitterly. For the first time I had witnessed the ways of insidious man who, in the name of economy and the development of our natural resources, has the penchant for destroying all that is aboriginal. Yet, all the while he wrings his hands and agonizes that there no longer exists that which he has just destroyed.

Dad assured me that the other rivers—the broad Susquehanna and the Delaware, about which he had told me so much—were not foul, at least where we would be fishing and that the Lackawanna had been dead for years for as long as he could remember, even before 1890. As always, I accepted his words, but the trauma of seeing that blackened river has never been erased. It has remained vivid even into the autumn of my years.

At such a young age the rationale that man is purely an economic creature meant nothing and my thoughtful father did not stress it, certain that I would learn only too soon about the paradox of spewing filth into the waters of our land then cursing that they no longer are fit to drink from and contain no fish. The Indians were most observant when they said about our way of plowing and planting: "White man make garden upside down." I am certain there must have been another saying: "White man throw own slop in spring."

The grindstone of time has worn away the keeness of some of the recollections of that cross-country journey, but there were many experiences to come. One does a lot of fishing in half a century.

I am contented that my father returned "home" as he put it. For it was in the woods and forests of Pennsylvania; in its rivers, mountains and pastoral streams, sometimes many miles and years removed but all the more hallowed for it, that I really learned the ways of the rod and gun. Under his tutelage and later that of other great outdoorsmen, whose secrets and skills I still try to emulate, I became something of a sportsman.

Eventually I put away the guns to concentrate on fishing. One day an enthusiastic young man mistook me for a cock pheasant and the load of number 6 shot that peppered my gun side left marks for years. But the flyrods in my study are cleaned, their reel seats and line guides oiled—always at the ready. They are not my servants; rather am I theirs. For when the rigors of business become untenable, one will beckon, and I take it from the rack and go a'fishing.

The Little Delight Makers

I am sure there is; but if there isn't, there should be an expression: "Wherever there's a bluegill or a perch, you'll find a boy." For the mystery of the hunt born in most, if not all boys, is probably first sensed along the banks of a perch or bluegill hole. It is there that each succeeding generation discovers anew its first quarry, and this is a most important stage in the process of growing up.

In time the bluegills, the crappies, the yellow perch, the catties of the miller's pond and the white perch of the salt marsh become replaced with the trout, salmon and bass, the stripers and marlin on which those same boys, now men, spend fortunes to pursue and write volumes about. But the "sunny" and perch that go with the stubbed toe are special breeds apart, for they are the little delight makers, the twigs that incline man's fishing tree.

I spent my ninth year on a large farm near Hawley, not far from the old Gravity Railroad in Wayne County, Pennsylvania. The winter had been bitterly cold, especially to a youngster just arrived from California, and endlessly long. When it finally yielded to the soft greening of spring I was quick to escape my cocoon of clothes and those felt-lined boots I was compelled to wear. Spring meant chores which at first I welcomed until one early April morning the sights of a busy, flicking phoebe and a lonesome worm exploring the reviving, sweet-smelling earth dictated otherwise. The thoughts of chores vanished when I stealthily picked up the worm, for I remembered what Jeb had told me so often at school that winter about the big, fat sunnies in the mill pond that bit like mad come May, then a long three weeks to wait.

Jeb was the miller's son. I liked him because, unlike the others, he did not refer to me as the "new kid from California" but seemed interested in what I knew about fishing. Naturally, I related at great length my experiences fishing "from coast to coast" when my parents moved from Los Angeles. That enthralled Jeb.

The farm where I lived was several miles from Jeb's house which adjoined the mill, and we had no opportunity to visit during the winter. Once his father came to the farm to discuss business with Frank and Clint, the two brothers who owned it. While they talked oats, Jeb and I talked fishing. Jeb approved of my little steel flyrod and brass reel, which were always cleaned and oiled, as suitable for the fish in the millpond; but when he spied the two ragged-out trout flies mixed with the little black hooks and split-shot sinkers spilling out of one of Dad's Prince Albert tobacco tins, he said: "Them's no good." And he licked one with his tongue. "Ain't no meat taste to it . . . tastes like rust." Then he made an ugly face. "Grubs is better."

Jeb always smelled like hay and the grain of his father's mill. He helped with bagging and sorting and knew how to change the belt drive that ran off the high-speed shaft. In the spring his father let him plow and disc their nearby small farmland with the new Fordson tractor, a snorting monster that could pull like an Erie freight engine. But over and beyond his many duties for a boy, Jeb had a fascinating enterprise all his own: his store—a little bench and wooden cabinet occupying a corner of the second level of the mill where the white oak floor had become honed smooth from the grain bags dragged over it for more than a century.

Jeb kept hooks; bobbers that he whittled, sanded and painted green and white, and split-shot sinkers, all securely padlocked in his cabinet until store time, after school. The hooks he sold three for a penny, the bobbers by size for either a nickel or a dime, the sinkers cost six cents for a barrel somewhat smaller than a shotgun shell. He had an uncommon sense of merchandising and I, of course, became his most loyal patron, within the limits of my chore money.

The Little Delight Makers

Jeb supplemented his store enterprise with a spectrum of live bait that included about everything that wriggled or twitched, from grubs to nightcrawlers which I helped him capture at every opportunity.

Jeb kept the worms, nightcrawlers and grubs in long, narrow cheese boxes. The crawlers were fed coffee grounds which must have satisfied them for they thrived in the moss and strips of burlap in those cheese boxes. What fun it was to lift the lid slowly to see them snap like released rubber bands into their holes and out of sight. For awhile Jeb fed the little red worms coffee grounds but they became so exhuberant about it that they sometimes wriggled themselves in half, especially those ringed ones that came from manure piles.

The grasshoppers—big yellow and green fellows that darted with the speed of a buzzing arrow—were hard to catch except in the morning before the sun had lifted the dew. Then they lay motionless as a twig, easy picking for a boy's deft fingers. I had helped Jeb make a box from an old screen door for housing the hoppers. Despite our many attentions, the hoppers were lethargic, and I doubt that they fed on the grass and meal we gave them.

The grubs came from the roots and stumps of what remained of an ancient and abandoned peach orchard. Of all the natural baits, Jeb conceded the grub was best. "The harder they are ta git, the better the fish like 'em," he said, and at the time his statement made sense.

Jeb had a very special, secret place for catching the biggest bluegills and sunnies in the pond: a gnarled stump big as a washtub about 12 feet from the shore. He reached the stump with a long plank he kept hidden in the bushes. The day he revealed his secret place to me he said: "This is it. All folks hafta have secrets and this is mine." I had to promise I would never tell anyone about it, and I have kept my word until now.

What sunnies and bluegills we caught! Flyrodders of today would give a spare reel to catch fish like those monsters. They were gluttons for the grubs from the old peach orchard. Teetering on Jeb's magic plank we hauled in perhaps the biggest sunnies of our fishing careers, some measuring well over 10 inches. And they fed continuously, at times accepting almost any reasonable bait, and some not so reasonable, like a piece of pressed ham slivered from a sandwich.

The very largest were selective, refusing the remnants of a worm or grub left on the hook by one that got away. As Jeb pointed out, "They ain't big fer nuthin." Then he showed me how to coax them into plucking a fresh grub by moving it ever so slowly between the snags and roots of the stump, a technique which I have never forgotten and use today with wet flies and nymphs.

So memorable that spring and summer! So indelible, but short. My family moved before the following winter in the interest of my father's business, and I never saw Jeb again. I suspect he became the miller in time, in spite of all his enterprising.

The twig had been further bent and as it inclined the tree, so had my search for sunnies and bluegills gone on. I found them the next spring in company with the yellow perch and a few skinny pickerel in the old and even-

The Little Delight Makers

then-overgrown canal flanking the Susquehanna not far from our home. They were cooperative as usual, although I could find no old peach orchard in whose roots hid the magic grub. But they did take the grasshoppers and crickets kicking three feet below the green and white bobber Jeb had given me before I left.

Neither time nor place have made any difference, for the bluegills spring eternal nearly everywhere. A few years later I learned to take them on the dry fly over their spawning beds and found them delightfully fond of Light Cahills and palmer-tied Gray Hackles. With a sharp "spat!" they would suck down the fly as if there never would be another, and I sharpened my budding skills—whatever they were at that age—for handling trout with the flyrod that were yet to come.

One hot, early May day on Spring Lake the bottom of the skiff was literally covered with bluegills that had taken the fly so avidly there was no time for stringing them. That was a Light-Cahill day. When my partner, a worm fisherman, saw me knotting on a dropper fly, he threatened to throw me out of the skiff. We had been working the shoreline which was laced with roots, windfalls and undergrowths such that casting was necessarily reckless, if the fly were to drop in the pockets where the bluegills were—on the far side of the windfalls. When one "spatted" the fly, its capture was largely luck.

Doubtless the largest bluegill I have ever hooked, or likely ever will hook, took the Light Cahill that day on Spring Lake. A gust had lifted the cast and deposited it into a pocket that I could never have hoped to reach by skill alone. The hackles had hardly touched before there was a loud splat like a spring-loaded shingle slapping the surface. There was no need to strike. After making a series of circles that kept the little rod thrumming, the bluegill broke tradition and became airborne. And for an instant my partner and I stared transfixed at the antics of that bluegill. We estimated it exceeded 13 inches. I gladly would have swum ashore and run all the way to the nearest taxidermist, had I boated it.

Imagine the show put on by one of three pounds that has just smacked your fly! The chances are you will never hook one that size, and if you did, I seriously doubt you would ever bring it to the net. A three-pounder (hypothetical, of course) tied tail to tail to a smallmouth bass of the same weight, in my opinion would drown the bass. And I believe the smallmouth is, as Henshall said, the gamest fish that swims.

All but one of the sunfish clan hanker for hackles and fur. The redear sunfish of the south, known in most places as the "shellcracker" for its preference for snails, stands apart when it comes to the fly. But the rock bass, warmouth, red breast, sunfish, crappie and even the little green sunfish, once called the only sunfish of the prairies, will gnaw the hackles off your best flies in a way that will delight you.

Many are the big-eyed rock bass that have snatched the White Miller at dusk at the mouth of Tunkhannock Creek. But alas, their spirit soon was gone and after a short tug or two they were on their side, quick subject for the landing net. But they are foolers! They associate with

The Little Delight Makers

the hard-hitting and long-fighting smallmouth bass, inhabiting the same pools and riffles, taking the same flies. In this sense, the rock bass is like the dace which, thinking it is a trout, acts like one, often rising beautifully to pluck the fly intended for the trout it thinks it is. But the rock bass for its gregariousness makes for pleasant hours in the life of a youth. It responds so well to all the thingamajigs in the flybook that boys invent: bewhiskered creations of all colors—a red feather here, two yellow ones there, a sprig of this and a little of that—all crowded together until there is hardly room to tie off the head. But the rock bass is not fussy. He will accept those early ties as quickly as those from the practiced fingers of a master. I loved him for that!

Crappies grow big on Maryland's Eastern Shore where the daily pulse of the Chesapeake in rivers like the Transquaking and Chicamacomico keep their waters brackish. Where the river bends to form a deep pool, the crappies await the sight of a twitching fly. How they smacked the Yellow May worked among the debris caught in the slowly turning eddies. I still have the drawing of one I caught there with the notes and a color legend for a final rendering that I never had time to finish. It was exactly 12 9/16 inches long, not a bad crappie. In those days I was concerned with such things as spine count, the shape of fins, characteristics of the gill flap and the like, the better to identify what I had caught, and I notice that the drawing has a note pointing to the spines of the dorsal fin: "six spines—same as in anal." And in the title block are recognizable erasures where I had first labeled the fish pomoxis *nigromaculatus* instead of the proper *pomoxis annularis.* So for a *white* crappie, the length of 12 9/16 is all the more impressive.

I have often written of the Chesapeake because there is so much to be said about it—the Eastern Shore, particularly. And there is evidence the shore's renowned resistance to change is being eroded. Developers riding bareback on the horse of expediency will have changed the tranquil scene of the "bugeye" and the crabbers boat before many years have passed. The new will replace the old, and with it, the fishing. Selfishly I resent the impending change, but it is inevitable.

I first met the white perch in the tidal creeks of the Chesapeake. I had been wading the edge of the marsh in search of stripers and testing the waist-deep water with a small double spinner and streamer, the best "hunting" lure I know. The tide had begun to ebb an hour earlier, and the current was ideal for working the little spinnered streamer around the grassy mounds and sand spits. But casting had become mechanical for no fish had shown.

In time a solid strike off a sand spit brought the rod tip down sharply. *Striper,* I thought. But after a brief tussle, I netted not a striper, but a chunky white perch, mean-eyed, stickle-finned and ornery. Hardly moving from my tracks, I took at least a dozen more, each like the other and close to a foot long. I did not know then that those perch were no youngsters. It was not until years later that I learned a perch eight years old may measure only nine or ten inches and weigh three-quarters of a pound.

The white perch is a spirited little fish. In the fall it will

The Little Delight Makers

test your lightest fly tackle with surprising vigor and sharpen your zeal for next spring's trout. At times it will take the dryfly but prefers the wetfly fished among the snags and along the banks. Like all panfish, the white perch is seldom longer than 12 inches. But the majority of trout one catches are not that long! At least three times a season I fish the Palmer River's upper reaches for the white perch. They like the wet fly in September and after the first frost. The river is clearer then, the weather crisp and the fish are quick to strike.

The largest yellow perch I ever boated was a fluke because it should have been a walleye. Dad and I were trolling in Lake Wallenpaupack with flyrods for walleyes. We had found a school and soon had four or five of the milky-eyed pike in the fish bag. After the strikes ceased, I turned the boat in a large loop to retrace our fading wake, holding the rod butt between my knees as I rowed.

Soon Dad's rod whipped down from the thrust of another walleye, and in moments my rod was bowed. Dad netted his fish first. It was a carbon copy of the others in the fish bag. But whatever was surging on my line kept boring. As it yielded to the rod, a huge yellow perch, bright as a Durham Ranger, flashed six feet down in the glass-clear water. Minutes later it lay in the landing net, humpbacked, deep-bellied, a fine specimen. Dad taped it at 16 inches; little shorter than our walleyes, but heavier. Never since have I caught or even seen such a yellow perch. Our small, weighted June Bug spinners and night-crawlers draped on number two, long-shank hooks probably were just above the thermocline to which the larger

yellow perch may descend. And, contrary to our expec-
tations, the fish proved to be a male.

Because I frequently fish for pickerel, I often pick up
sizeable perch. They seem to occupy the same waters. But
none has yet approached the size of that one from Lake
Wallenpaupack in 1933.

The Little Huntington is pastoral for the several miles it
weaves through the foothills below Jonestown, Pa. Being
rather small above its confluence with Fishing Creek at
Forks, it has the character of a trout stream which, in
several stretches, it is. The river is idyllic, and I have spent
many fulfilled hours casting for smallmouths with
number six McGintys in the darkness of its pools. The
bass were seldom over a foot long, but they were always
able to account for themselves from the moment they felt
the barb until they rested in the landing net. The Huntington was blessed with an abundance of crawdads, the
real bread and butter of the smallmouth, and the bass
showed it by their stocky bodies and spring-tailed dispo-
sitions.

I first knew of the power of attraction the McGinty has
for the smallmouth when C. Jim Pray, master tier of flies
of Eureka, California, sent me several that had proved so
successful for steelhead. At once I recognized their po-
tential for smallmouth. The full, typically short squirrel
wing, brown deer-body hackle, yellow and black banded
body, the teal and red tail whisks, and the beautifully
placed jungle cock eyes comprised a smallmouth fly if I
ever saw one. And the McGinty worked. Dropped at the

The Little Delight Makers

foot of the riffles to swing slowly among the rocks in the long pools, it fetched bass like a grub lures a sunfish.

In October the little river was low and clear as pure glass. Then the bass would venture into the pockets quite like brown trout questing for nymphs and minnows. What days! By then most anglers would have switched to the shotgun, and rarely was there a rod working the pools but mine. Careful wading was in order and the cast had to drop ever so softly, for even 2X tippets seemed coarse as crochet thread. The Huntington was a chapter in itself. It revealed its secrets reluctantly over the seasons and in learning them I garnered lore that proved so useful wherever I cast the fly for smallmouth; principally that they can be as selective as any trout. In low, clear water the smallmouth is capable of discernment for which it seldom is given credit.

Long, upstream casts were one of the Huntington's secrets. Long, leaders tapered to 2X and tipped with the McGinty were another. And if the McGinty should fail to produce there was the third secret—that a double copper spinner and a long-shank Cahill cast upstream to wander back as it chose among the subtle currents would coax a strike or two.

Perhaps I appreciated the Huntington most for its predictability; I had such an affinity for it. Other rivers are of many moods and at times are strange, even unfriendly, but not the Huntington. I have not waded it in some years now, but I'd be surprised if the McGinty did not work as well today!

The Huntington was a joy to fish all season long, but it was during the autumns that I had come to know it best. October's frost would have turned the aspen into rare pageantry, the touch of Midas lingering on the curled leaves that gathered over the pools. Evening would settle quickly, and small night sounds would pervade the narrow valley. The weight on the creel webbing would be welcome, for once again the Huntington had been kind, and I would wade ashore, knowing all was well and mellowing in the peaceful and lonely quiet that speaks to those who wade the stream.

The Little Delight Makers

The River
Has a Way

For my tenth birthday my father gave me one of his most prized possessions, an English 10-foot fly rod with which he had taken native brook trout, bass, crappies, walleyes, pickerel, perch, and even creek suckers and catfish.

It was a veteran subtly showing the care it had received through the years: talltales of replacement windings that did not quite fill the old spaces, the worn away finish on the fittings from polishings, the patch of cork dust and glue in the grip to plug the gouge from the barb of a pickerel hook. Of course, no other rod could compare with that old masterpiece of bamboo, pinned ferrules, and sliding reel seat.

On that chilly October morning the mist wraiths of autumn pervaded the river valley. The ochers and russets of the chestnut and oak trees portended the season's end. And we could see, even in the gray of dawn, how clear was the river, how scoured and free from the summer's algae were the round stones.

"We'll get bass today, boy," Dad said. And I believed him.

With the wooden scoop and shivering like all boys shiver, I bailed the skiff, wishing that the fingers of the sun soon would reach across the river to pluck away the patches of fog hovering over the channel. Then I wiped the seats with the burlap fish bag, placed the bait bucket under the stern seat, the oars in their locks.

I picked up the already strung 10-footer from where it safely lay atop a swayback picnic table and took my place at the oars.

"No, son," Dad said. "Today is your day." And as he took the oars in his big hands, he smiled in a way I might not fully understand for many years.

I pushed us off, getting one foot wet as I always did, and slithered to the stern seat. Dad eased the boat into the current. "Hook the stone catty through both lips." he said. "And cast it gently upstream." I accomplished that feat with difficulties peculiar to a boy's fingers. We drifted, letting the current dictate our course, a practice I had learned was good. "The river has a way," Dad said. "It will take you to the best places, it you let it. And it will tell you about the fish, if you listen.

The brightness of morning began to touch the tall trees

The River Has a Way

fringing the cliff on the far side of the river. A few remaining mallards had commmenced their business of the day, the silent drakes moving subtly amidst the ruffling hens who remonstrated in bickering chorus. Some thrummed for a moment to skitter away in pairs, to feed elsewhere, or to carry on with what ducks do on chilly October mornings.

Far down the river the faint rumble of the Lehigh Valley westbound, followed by the sharp authority of its whistle, echoed up the river, the sounds gradually becoming transcended by the bark of the big Pacific's exhaust, drumming the cadence for the whirling drivers. And as it sped by, I marveled at the way of man and machine and concluded at that moment that the most important things in life were a throttle, a whistle cord and a 10-foot fly rod. Dad explained how, as a boy, he had watched the old camelbacks of his youth snort and moan over those same tracks.

"You could see light between the drivers and the inside rails," he said. "Especially when McGrath was on the throttle and running late." He added, "It's good for fishing, you know. The noise stirs up the bass."

We drifted toward the cleft where the river divided quietly, the skiff taking the far side. "Get ready," Dad said. "There's a deep hole coming up—over there where the water is dark. You should feel one soon—when we're over the eddy."

In a few moments a strong tug, followed quickly by several more, set the 10-footer twitching. The line swished through the guides. "Now!" Dad said in a low voice, as if the running smallmouth might hear. I struck hard enough to nearly upset. Sixty feet astern my first smallmouth soared into the air, shaking so violently that the stone catty was hurled up the leader to the line knot. The old rod arched beautifully, pulsing with each lunge of the bass until, after what seemed all of fifteen minutes—but really was only two or three—Dad lifted the 16-inch bass into the skiff with his landing net.

It was a brilliant fish—olivaceous, darkly mottled above the lateral line, pearllike and brassy beneath the gill covers. Dad wet the burlap bag, slid the bass into it, then fastened the drawstring to the oarlock. "It's your turn," I said. And we exchanged places, to repeat at least four times before the sun was high overhead.

That day on the Susquehanna over forty-five years ago was the talisman of my fishing career. By today's standards that old 10-footer was, perhaps, cumbersome, as were the enameled lines, which remained coiled if the weather turned cold. And even then we knew that clear water meant light leaders, coiled Japanese gut that was "polished" until after it had been wet for a few hours when the polish turned a fuzzy white.

Getting the bait was almost as exciting as doing the fishing. All sorts of creatures would pass through the channels that we hoed in the creek bed in our quest for crawdads, hellgrammites, mud minnows, riffle pike, stone catties and "bass bugs"—nymphs of the dragonfly.

Some clung to the mosquito netting of the bamboo-legged seine, and Dad explained the mysteries of their metamorphoses: how they, as aquatic insects, spent nearly all of their lives underwater and how nature is perpetuated by such creatures subsisting on one another and fish on them, to effect a normal and necessary balance. And if the water became polluted, even invisibly, the nymphs, the larvae, the fish would be gone.

The insects I learned to draw and, with modest success, to render in water color. And it was natural, I expect, to turn to imitating them with fur, feathers, quill, even some highly coveted objects from my mother's Sunday hat.

The next Christmas I was given my first hip boots—big, black, straight as a pair of pants and fluted up the legs, oblique at the tops. In one foot was hidden a box containing a dozen flies discovered when I tried to put my foot into the boot. Overjoyed with the boots, I was utterly fascinated with those beautiful Scotch flies, dressed on Spanish silkworm gut snells and aligned between the two aluminum combs in the bottom of the box like tiny soldiers in a company front. I remember them well: the Royal Coachman, the Wickham's, the Queen of the Waters, the Ginger Quill, the ragged Hare's Ear, the cup-winged Professor, the somber March Brown, the neat little Cahill, and some English duns.

It was so long until April, I thought. And I knew we would be using worms then anyhow. So I contented myself with taking the flies from the box, to examine that which to me was the legerdemain of all artistry, the tying of a fly. And as I preened their hackles and stroked their wings, I envisioned the gulping rises of great brown trout long as your arm, trout that only I, and no other anglers, knew existed.

April did come after painfully long waiting. And sure enough, for two weeks, we used the worms I had spaded from the vegetable garden. It was always too early for flies but never too early for putting in the onion sets. I had measured winter's slow passing by learning the arcanum of the whip finish for snelling worm gangs, the knot Dad insisted on for its wrapped-over end. And I spent many hours tying those gangs, carefully whipping them in red silk and coating them with exactly three coats of varnish.

May weather, too, was late that year. When it arrived, so did the floppy March Browns and the pert little Ginger Quills, their nymphs jerking to the surface to flutter into duns, the duns to return that afternoon as the glassy spinners so copied by fly anglers.

"Just wait until the spinners come back," Dad said. "Watch the trout then."

How those Ginger Quills danced, sweeping up and down over the dark pools, the trout boiling and leaping, eschewing all else. Pairs in copula would sail by, their egg sacs tiny sparks against the green of spring. And when released, the females would dip and rise, then dip again trying, before the trout had sipped them from sight, to extrude their progeny. Those that did not fell spent, to become lost among the dimples of the rising trout.

I had come to cast fairly well by then, had learned to wait for the tug of the backcast which despite my best efforts and the obedience of the ten-footer too often went out of control. And I knew how to shoot a little hook, if the flies were to drop softly before a rising trout. Little difference did it make if the fly should float or sink. Yet it took

The River Has a Way

another quarter of a century to learn that again, notwithstanding my later avidity for the hypotheses of Gordon, Steenrod, Halford, Gill, LaBranche, Hewitt, Jennings, and Bergman, whose writings continuously interfered with learning the declensions, conjugations, and absolutes of Latin.

The following winter I first collected feathers, wishing that I had kept the plumage from the mallards, grouse, and ringnecks from other autumns. Sooner or later all boy fishermen make their own flies and eventually become responsible for the moths eating holes in the best blankets, for the blood stains from bird skins and rabbit ears hidden in brown paper bags, for the indelibility of picric acid stains on towels and such, and for the howls from irate senior householders whose bare feet have a penchant for attracting lost fishhooks better than does any magnet.

But by artifice best known to boys who fish, I increased those precious acquisitions of feathers and hair until they and the smelly boxes and bags containing them all but drove my mother mad. The poor woman was always sniffing suspiciously under the bed, behind cabinets, in overcoat pockets and in the spare-room clothes closet.

Even Miss Whittecomb, my algebra teacher, was certain I had become a cigarette fiend, because of the residuals of picric acid on my fingers which she had misjudged to be tobacco stains.

Becoming a proponent of the wet fly was a rather natural tendency. My feathered inventions sank, and when I put together others with hackles almost as puffy as a dandelion, the better to make them float, they too sank. But strangely, some trout did not reject all of the feathered potpourri and were taken home, perhaps victims of film-fly technique, of which I knew nothing.

After dropping my bicycle on the driveway, I would grab my creel, dash into the house to expound at great length how I had outwitted each trout that I plopped in the sink, and gesticulating as only a 13-year-old can, demonstrate the exactness of the cast, the rise of the trout, the strike, and how each trout had bowed the old 10-footer into a fearful bend.

As the years so stealthily slipped away, years that for some strange reason I no longer measured by the times I had spaded the garden or witnessed the first of the March Browns and Ginger Quills, I realized that Dad and I had not been fishing together often. Twenty at the time, I had bought my first car, a second-hand Hupmobile. Having acquired new pursuits, I was home usually just to eat and sleep. That I rationalized, was the only reason for not fishing together more often. That, plus the seemingly endless demands of the job and college. But the fact that we had not been fishing together persisted.

It struck me hard one evening on Long's half-mile stretch, when I came upon him by chance. Approaching the big rock, which for centuries had diverted and muted the upper creek, I glanced up to see him sitting there watching me roll a cast of Cahills into the suds behind the rock. He waved, said nothing, smiled. The depression in his weathered jacket, from the weight of the creel strap, meant trout. Then I saw again the sag of his shoulders,

The River Has a Way

remembered the uncertainty of his vision, his tendency to nap more often.

A good trout flashed at the tail fly but did not take. I retrieved the line, waded to the point where I could cross, and walked to the rock where he sat. We talked for hours, it seemed. He was interested in my plans, how the job and school were going. And we talked about the youth thing in Germany, the Little Corporal, the Dolfuss slaying a few years earlier, the treaty of Versailles. I remembered his comment about Dolfuss when we first heard, that day on the Susquehanna, the day we rented the cabin, of Dolfuss's assassination: "Sounds like the Archduke Ferdinand all over again. But it's about that time . . . soon as the new crop is tall enough and strong enough, some political knothead will pull a stunt or maybe a ship will be sunk somewhere . . . and millions of the saplings will be cut down before they've had the chance to sprout leaves."

Once years before he had called my attention to a sparrow which, as we watched, repeated its song from each of the corners of his assumed domain. "He's telling other birds where his boundaries are," Dad said. "Generally they respect each other. But, look!" He pointed to an encroaching blackbird in the act of trying to elude the authoritative pecks from the pursuing, smaller sparrow. "Sometimes they don't," he added.

That was the day we had fished the South Branch for brook trout. The day had been hot, the creek thinned from endless timbering of the watershed. And he drove to the little general store at the fork for lunch. Later, he said, we would try the evening rise at Long's half mile.

"Ever had beer?" Dad asked. "No," I said. And he ordered two bottles of home brew and sandwiches planked with thick ham and cheese. At 16 I had become a man. I was drinking beer eye-to-eye with my father, a most pleasant experience, I discovered.

Strange that those recollections should come to me while we chatted that evening on the big rock. Stranger still, that I should remember them now.

Dad loaded his pipe, then said, "By the way, I caught four good browns on that big Cahill you tied for me when you were just starting." He plucked the well-mouthed fly from his hatband and handed it to me. "It's a good tie," he said. I detected pride in his voice.

Shortly after the holocaust of December Seventh I enlisted, then learned that orders to report for duty would be delayed for several months, pending quota requirements. The thoughts of spring meant March Browns and Ginger Quills; of the summer, stone catties and river bass, the old 10-footer and the skiff with the wet seat boards and the splintery bow. Mainly they meant the companionship of the kind gentleman who had shown me how to do those many things I so easily had come to accept for granted.

By telephone we talked of the river, the growing fad of spinning, the skiff, which had been swept away in the spring flood. But trout season was only three weeks old. We would spend a day together on Long's half mile before I entrained.

I found him there in the clearing asleep in the old car. His rod was strung and standing upright between the fender and the bumper. A March Brown rested in the

The River Has a Way

keeper ring. And in a moment after I had called his name, he put on his glasses, slipped into his waders and picked up his rod. "There's been a hatch," he said. "We should catch a trout or two."

He started at the foot of the lower pool where the footing was better for wading. I said I would wait awhile and follow on the opposite side. I really preferred to watch him once more; watch him roll those long, easy casts I once had envied but still respected . . . pickup . . . tug . . . roll—the fly a thistle nesting in the surface film.

I watched him progress slowly up the shallow side of the quiet pool, noticed that he stumbled when he waded. But soon his rod bowed to the surge of a good trout. Lifting the rod high overhead, which he had taught me to do, he sampled the trout's strength, then lowered the rod in response to the trout's demand for line. It *was* as good trout! How it bored and darted, slashed the surface, skittered cross current in the attempt to rid itself of the fraud pricking its mouth. And after eight minutes that trout was still performing the gyrations to free itself acquired from the experiences of past seasons.

In time I approached the sandy bar to which I knew Dad would lead the trout and waded quietly to a point where I could net it with one sure effort. I did carefully, after the trout rolled on its side. It was heavy in the net—a magnificent fish, broad, thick, brilliantly golden, spotted and opalescent—a male brown whose strong jaws one surely would think could divest such a small hook of its sting and be free of it.

Dad looked at the trout and then at me. "Let's release

it," he said. "He'll be around to catch again. Maybe when you've come home." And he looked away quickly.

The big trout lay on its side in the shallow pool where I had placed it, its fins fanning, mouth gaping. Gradually the movements quickened and the thick body rolled uncertainly upright, fell back, then righted itself again. The broad tail swept back and forth and in another moment the trout returned to the darkness of the deeper water from which it had come.

Dad saw me off the next day. "I'll have a new skiff by the time you are back," he said. And we shook hands then, something we had never done before, I suppose because we had never had occasion to.

I looked back to see him standing there, his smile taking me back to that day on the Susquehanna when, on my tenth birthday, he had given me one of his most prized possessions, a ten-foot fly rod. I have forgotten whatever became of it.

One spring evening when the March Browns and Ginger Quills are due I will revisit the half mile, now a long drive from home. The big brown, of course, no longer will be there. I suspect he became the arch prize, one mid-April morning of a shivering, skinny boy who, with a snelled hook draped with a fat garden worm or two gathered from an onion bed, derricked that trout into history. I like to think so.

Come that evening, and because I have heard it is so, I will see how much the scene has changed and paled; how askew and warped the creek has become from the concrete rinks of the freeway. And if there are no signs of

The River Has a Way

rising trout, no hatches of mayflies whose bodies are bright against the green of spring, I will not wonder why.

My two sons may meet me there. But they have their first cars now; and between the rigors of college and their jobs they are seldom home except to sleep and eat. So far they have not received orders to report for duty. Maybe they will meet me there. I like to watch them cast: pickup . . . tug . . . roll—the fly a thistle gliding to the surface.

If they are late, I just might have a can of beer, might even have a nap while I wait. . . .

Nev, a Very
Special Fisherman

In our time of the ego merchant, the exploiter and the headline hunter, some may find it difficult to accept that there ever were men, really great in their fields, who did not seek to become famous or even known. Rather did they perform their skills, however acquired, in a way pleasant to them, preferring satisfaction from sheer achievement to the huzzahs of publicity. So it was and, to some extent, still is among some of the fishing greats. I have known many of them, probably some of the most skillful, analytical and productive anglers ever to cast to a rising fish. Yet, you may never have heard or read of them.

I doubt that the one I write about had ever explored the works of the renowned writers, fishing or otherwise, or even had access to them. The only fishing book I knew him to have was an old, borrowed, broken-backed Walton, the one with the illustration of the sinker with an integrally cast eye in the upper end. As his own innovator he was really more enmeshed with his own discoveries than with the popular theorems of those who, prolific with words, bend the mind to the customs of the times.

Perhaps his most refreshing quality was his absolute pragmatism: using what he had, coveting not the latest —especially if he did not have it—holding his own skills above the idolatry of gadgetry. And for such he was indeed a singular performer and man, an unforgettable traditionalist, I suppose.

If I learned the ways of the trout from him, I learned far more about fishing, particularly fishing the river of life. "Gather in your line if you've missed," he would say. "Take out the knots and cast again, and again, as many times as you must, until you've made your strike. But keep on until you do."

And I guess that is what it's all about.

I first met Nev on the Wapwallopen many years ago when that river was esteemed for its salmon-size brown trout. That is, I heard him before I saw him; heard his purple monologue resounding through the little valley before I came upon him standing thigh deep in a fast run, snorting and bawling eight-syllable cusswords which, I learned later, were directed to the sliding ring on his reel seat. It had slipped, freeing his reel which fell into the tail of the run where he stood, moments after he had buried the barb of his Professor in the jaw of a heavy trout.

There he stood, flailing the air in the attempts to hold onto the trout and recover the line peeling from the reel. Handicapped as he was, he did well. His performance, if only for not falling in, was remarkable, and I was taken with his unusual facility for having what seemed three hands: one for reaching to the stripping guide to yank back loose line; another for holding the rod high; and yet another for stuffing between his teeth the yards of line he somehow managed to gather from behind him.

Nev continued his tirade with artfully punctuated, never-forgotten syllabic emphasis. But in time he concluded the episode, skillfully bringing the big trout to net and tossing it, safely enmeshed, into the thick grass fringing the bank. Still sputtering and jerking his head up and down like a chicken pecking corn, he began the task of recovering his reel, first setting his rod in the crotch of a spruce, then retrieving the line, hand over hand, until the reel lay at his feet.

He simmered at this point, except for an occasional blurt, to show the patience with which fishermen paradoxically seemed endowed, and started to put things aright with his neckerchief, screwdriver, oil thimble, and mucilin.

I believed it safe to approach but hesitated a little. Then as I drew near to the man, I became intrigued with his hat. It was pointed, after the fashion of Robin Hood's and embellished with the full-length feather from, in Nev's

Nev, a Very Special Fisherman

case, a cock pheasant. No less intriguing was his fishing vest obviously culled from a well-weathered hunting coat from which he had removed the sleeves, probably long since shredded by barbed wire and the briars of many hunts.

When he became aware of the crunch of my boots on the gravel, he whirled about, commanding: "Don't step on that line!! The ___ ___ _____ reel fell off and I'm trying to set up again. Besides, there's one hell of a trout about six feet below the end of that big _____ flat rock. So walk quiet!"

I stepped back a pace or two, while he eyed me for a moment. Then he grinned, asking: "What are you using?"

"A Wickham's," I said, certain he would disapprove.

"That's all right, lad. It's all right ... it'll work. It's a good pattern for now. Me? I like the Professor."

I stood there watching the feather in his hat quiver while he struggled with his line. Then we both heard the trout he mentioned boil as it came up for a fly. Immediately he looked at the spot behind the rock then back at me. "Well, don't stand there," he bawled. "There's a trout to be caught! Get your tail over there where I told ya and have at it. You don't catch trout unless you're fishin'."

For some reason I wanted to show this man that I knew how to handle a rod, maybe demonstrate that I had caught a few trout in my short years. So I waded carefully to a safe place where the strong current mended behind a submerged boulder. From there, I figured, after two or three false casts, I might be able to drop the Wickham's into the pocket just upstream of the big brown; that is, if the too-light line I was using would not jackknife for want of follow-through.

Feeling Nev's eyes following my every move, I let fly in my best style which, in those years, was not very elegant, but the trout rose on schedule for the Wickham's. Everything else went awry and sure enough, the line jackknifed from too much loop. I missed the strike but did feel that disheartening, slight fadeaway tug of a trout that had escaped the barb.

Immediately I heard Nev's foghorn expostulations that I needed lessons on "handling that nice rod and should learn something about keeping a tight line in strong current." Knowing that the trout was down for hours, I abashedly waded ashore to where Nev sat. He had just put his gear in order from his mishap and sat there drawing hard on a hand-turned cigarette.

"It happens to all of us, sometimes," he said quietly. "But I noticed you don't push your rod hard enough. Next time push it all the way until it's horizontal." He grinned. "Are you afraid of breaking it? You won't."

And thereupon began a long period of tutoring at no expense to anyone but Nev, for his patience. For many seasons he taught me the way of the trout; schooled me about flies and how to recognize the real from the fanciful and how to tie flies that looked like flies. When he showed me how to gauge Spanish silkworm gut and tie leaders, he said, "Dye them in strong tea, they'll have the shades of being touched by the sun."

One time he revealed his very private trick for fixing a

Nev, a Very Special Fisherman

dryfly that would bring up browns in slow, clear water: singeing the bottom of the hackle with a cigarette. "Most hackle is too damn big, too long," he said. "Big, wise trout often push the fly away, if the hackle is in the way. But the little fellows are like suction pumps. The braggin' trout sip a bug easy, and if they mouth hackle that is too long and wiry, the fly will spring free. Or maybe the trout let go ... I dunno." He paused for a moment, puffing on his brown-stained cigarette. "The best dryfly for a brown, a big one that is, is a wetfly ... with just a little mucilin rubbed in it," he said. He rubbed his thumb and forefinger together. "Just enough mucilin to keep the fly on top."

As the seasons passed, I realized that I had caught more trout, that whatever casting style I had had become better purely from watching Nev and listening to him cuss me out when I did foolish things. And of all the so-called rules Nev taught me, the most intangible was doubtless the most productive: synchronizing the false cast with the measured rhythm of a rising trout. "What's the good of having your fly three feet behind the trout when he's ready to take a fly he's seen coming toward him?" he would query. "Watch the trout for awhile and time its rise by counting, then have at it."

He would cock his good eye on me and ask, "Did you hear what I just said?" And as I nodded my head, he would say, "Learn the rhythm. Big ones don't get big by accident. Learn that and you'll time your cast just right. That is, if you can learn to cast where you're looking." And he would grin, showing his chipped tooth.

His lantern jaw and Popeye forearms made him appear

so much larger than his 150 pounds, but when he fixed his good eye on you, you knew you were looked at. Then he seemed all of eight feet tall. Nev's other eye had been left sightless from a steel chip before he was thirty. Sometimes he would say it really was not a steel chip that had blinded that eye but a size ten Professor (with just a little mucilin on it) spit back at him by a monstrous brown trout "nearly four feet long."

A master of the double entendre, Nev had a way with words, once heard, never forgotten. For his philosophies were often colored with questioning near humor. Once he said over his shoulder, after he had waded beyond his boot tops: "Sometimes fishing with a wet fly means fishing with a wet backside, too."

On occasion he would shift into a bit of ventriloquism, playing the role of Joe, a legendary trout that even Nev could not catch. Peering down into the depths of the pool, Nev might call, "Hey, Joe, what's the fly today?" Then, cupping his ear, he would listen attentively to the gurgling voice seeming to come from the very bottom of the pool. "Stonefly," it would say. And Nev would chuckle as he looked at the stonefly in his keeper ring. "See what I mean? And Joe is always right."

I knew better than to ask why he had never caught Joe, the prophetic trout.

Nev had an old Model-T Ford Tudor equipped with a special intermediate gear which gave it the ability to climb hills at a faster clip than it could from the foot-pedal low gear. For some reason only he knew, Nev would whistle softly whenever he pulled the black-knobbed

Nev, a Very Special Fisherman

shift lever into that magic intermediate gear. The Ford would buzz in a different key and surge ahead, triumphantly gaining as much as five miles an hour.

That flivver whinnied and jerked, season after season, through the big wilds of Pennsylvania, leaving its hose-like tracks in incredible places. Sure footed as a goat, it was obedient to every demand Nev made of it—on the road or off. Even the heavy snows of deer season did not deter it, for Nev could jockey, tease and manipulate that old machine into places meant only for animal tracks, not those of a skinny-wheeled Ford. At such times he would instruct me in the mysteries of the three pedals for rocking in deep drifts.

Once the Ford had become stuck nearly axle deep in the swale bordering the wider reaches of the Loyalsock. Working the three pedals like he was playing a pipe organ and whistling at the shift lever, Nev "see-sawed" the Ford to firmer ground in short order. "I'll drive this fool car all the way to the gates of heaven," he chortled. "Maybe I won't get in! But if there isn't good fishin' there, I'll turn around and come back anyhow."

Years later when mired in jungle muck, I wished for that old flivver and, to this day, believe it would have whinnied and grunted its way through that near morass, despite its tires no bigger than a small boy's arm.

Nev kept assorted snelled hooks in the little flower vase clamped to the right door post. On rough road they would dance and clink, sometimes springing free to scatter the remnants of worms from the last night of catfishing dried hard as a scorched noodle.

Nev's flyrod was the paragon of hand-split tonkin with closely-spaced intermediate wrappings of silk, which were then the style. It was a story in itself, for it was composed of odd sections he had accumulated through the years from damaged rods brought to him for repairs. "People throw away many good things nowadays," he would say. "It's almost cheaper to buy anything new instead of fixing what you have—something that's treated you well and you like. Like a good rod." And he would flick his rod back and forth in admiration of its full sweep. "F'rinstance, I steamed and re-glued two sections of this one. The other section, the butt, was good; just scraped it down a little to slow down the action. I've had this rod for over twenty years and it's never let me down."

With that rod Nev caught everything with fins within several hundred miles, wherever the Ford would take him. And, like the profound Walton who relished a mixed bag, Nev was never above changing his gear to fiddle with the lesser fishes, bluegills and even chubs, should he find them surfacing at the breast of a dam or in a deep eddy. On many a July evening I watched him slogging downstream toward camp or the appointed meeting place dangling big brown trout, smallmouth and pickerel, too large to creel, on a rawhide lace tied to his belt. I never knew Nev to use another rod.

Known only to his relatively few intimates, Nev was a sort of loner, spending much of his time pumping a flyline over the creeks and rivers he loved so well. At times he was asked to guide well-dollared people who hoped to experience the feel of their first trout. One time he carried

Nev, a Very Special Fisherman

a minister piggyback across the swollen waters of Fishing Creek and later laughed, "Ministers have been on my back for years about my cussing, but that fellow didn't say a word."

Nev was janitor at the local elementary school, and he had a little workshop in the basement where he tied flies and fussed with rods. For many hours I watched him sort his hackles, wings, floss and quills, marvelling at the unbelievable delicacy with which his coarse hands caressingly set the wings of his Professors, Gingers, Cahills and Gordons.

"Why settle for anything less than perfect," he would say. "Suppose it does take me 15 or 20 minutes to tie a fly! When it's finished, it's right. At least it suits me." And when he tossed one in the air, he would smile as the fly alighted upright with a barely perceptible "tick" atop his long work bench. "See that shadow. Notice how the wings slant back a little. That's what a trout looks for." Then he might hand me the fly and say, "Put it in your flybox. It may come in handy one day."

Regrettably, I have not a single fly Nev so carefully dressed. Those I once had somehow escaped in the jaws of a trout or became lost in history.

Nev never wrote a book. What an enrichment of the fishing literature it would have been, if he had! I have yet to find in the lore of our contemporaries certain of his knowledge that he absorbed from his countless days astream. And I suppose that any editor would have needed a very blue pencil to line out the purple of Nev's expression.

He may not have been judged a reflective man by those who did not know him well, but he was exactly that. "The woods are my church," he would muse. "I can sit in any pew I like and say it the way I want to."

Once he paid me a compliment: "I like you because you talk with your ears." From Nev that was quite a statement. Something like getting an A in chemistry.

I remember so well the sight of his hand-warped Robin Hood hat and his old sleeveless hunting jacket bulging with trout and bobbing up and down, as he hustled on to the next pool out of sight. Once there, and with the finesse of the impresario, he was sure to have his way with the trout . . . because he knew theirs.

I often reflect on that day on the Loyalsock when he wrestled his flivver out of the swale and said, "I'll drive this fool car to the gates of heaven." Doubtless he did. With the special gear the Ford probably got there on time. And when he approached the last check point, surely the Great Warden smiled kindly upon him and let him pass through—Nev, his Robin Hood hat with the pheasant feather, the whinnying Ford and all—to that place where very special trout are seen only by very special fishermen. Like Nev.

Nev, a Very Special Fisherman

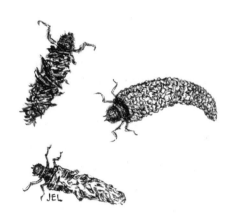

A Night for the Caddis

I learned my first stream lore back in the days when an entomologist was a fellow who prevented borers and weevils from destroying the farmers' crops. Books on entomology for the angler then were few, except for some of the British classics, and the flyrodder had to gather bits of knowledge as best he could simply by fishing or by following the footsteps of older, experienced anglers. One's own research evolved from the natural course of events, regardless of how he went about it.

Anglers then may not have known the orders of insects, but they knew the mayflies, caddisflies and stoneflies that abounded in their streams and rivers; when they would emerge, how long the hatches would last, how to tie and use flies that represented the naturals. Yet the words Ephemeroptera, Trichoptera and Plecoptera were meaningless to most and seldom, if ever, heard. Doubtless few would have raised an eyebrow to learn that their old, dependable March Brown was really the *Stenonema vicarium* or that the Blue Quill—sometimes the Black Quill—was actually the *Epeorus pleuralis* or *Iron fraudator* for which Theodore Gordon's quill pattern became so celebrated.

They knew how to tie and fish wetflies—arts which in later years became all but lost in the rise of interest for the dryfly and nymph. Wetfly fishing was little short of worm dunking; or so said the proponents of the dryfly. It was just another bit for the history books on angling.

There were more trout then because there were more back-country streams to support them. Pollution had not reached its peak (Will it ever?), and the watersheds were not yet gone. Fishing the wetfly in fast water was simply the matter of wading downstream and teasing the trout along the way with a dropper and a tail fly. Rods were longer, and it was right that they were. They were perfect for "hanging" the flies in a pool with little, if any, drag. Mine was a 9½-footer with an action considered soft by today's standards. With it, after a season or two, I had learned to "wig-wag" the dropper fly across the surface by gently pulsing the rod tip against the anchoring effect from the larger, deeper-swimming tail fly. That was sheer magic for coaxing brook trout from behind a rock.

Methods, styles and patterns of flies have changed in-

A Night for the Caddis

evitably since then. Yet the effectiveness of the wet fly has remained unchanged for those who believe in it. Here I mean the *winged* wetfly in patterns almost as old as the fishhook, itself, not the elegant nymphs of today that everyone seems to fancy. There was and there is a place for the Cahill, the Queen of the Waters, the Grouse and Green, the Teal and Yellow, the Woodcock and Orange, and that place is right on the end of your leader, if you know when and how to use them. But that's the secret, as with all things about fish and fishing.

Clint Thatcher taught me wetfly fundamentals. He handed down the basics for fishing the wetfly and the details for tying it correctly. Clint was a Canadian. We met in the early '30s below the old iron bridge that crossed Fishing Creek above Benton. The stream deepened there and became canal-like. It was wadable in only a few places, particularly in early May. Shrouded in the sha-dows of the hemlock growing to its very edge, the water was always dark.

A hard shower had driven me under a dripping tree where I crouched, soaked to the bone, watching for signs of feeding trout. But the stream surface had become a blanket of bright buttons of rain, and I would see nothing beneath it until the rain had stopped many minutes later. Then eight or ten brown trout, big as cordwood in two rows, appeared in the sunlight spearing through the dense shrouds of the hemlock. One after another would tack into the current to flash for a nymph or pupa, then return to its orderly position, finning the water easily in wait for the next insect to come into view. From where I crouched, I could not discern what the insects were for none had yet emerged.

Clint appeared from out of nowhere from the opposite bank, and after a brief pause slipped into the waist-deep water as stealthily as a muskrat. He stood quietly, his rod at the ready, several loops of line in his left hand. He was far enough downstream not to disturb the trout which continued to pluck the nymphs rising nearer to the surface as the minutes passed.

A trout bulged the surface and Clint moved his rod only twice to stretch his first cast. His leader rolled out to settle like a gentle mist, the fly barely dimpling the surface six feet upstream from where the trout had bulged the water. I realized I was holding my breath because I was seeing what Clint could not: the trout feeding casually among the probing ribbons of light *and* the fly Clint so beautifully had cast above them.

The trout continued to roll out after a nymph here, another there. Because the current was slow, Clint's fly drifted for many seconds. For a moment I lost sight of his fly then spotted it again in a spear of light just before a trout in the first row flashed toward it. The fly disappeared. Clint hesitated for a split second, then struck with a slight flick of his wrist. He must have struck from instinct, I thought, because I was sure he could not have seen the trout take the fly.

The following minutes were a drama, indeed. From my vantage point under the hemlock, I watched both trout and trouter. It seemed Clint's trout at first was not disturbed for it leisurely began to return to its feeding position. Then when it felt the sinew of Clint's rod, it thrust upstream, to be joined by two other trout swimming beside it, all three darting and twisting as if yoked.

Suddenly the two departed and the remaining ones scattered. Only the hooked trout remained in sight, darting back and forth through the lattices of light. Clint's rod swept low time after time in rhythm with the lunges of the trout. With the touch of the master that he was, he let go and recovered line faultlessly, holding the nodding rod arched against the movements of the fish. And when the trout churned the surface in a furious boil, Clint pointed the rod low toward the water to keep the line tight.

The wisp of leader held, and finally Clint eased the trout nearer. He waited for it to make its last few rolls and darts then, at just the right moment, unsnapped the wood-bow landing net and led the trout head first into it.

"That was beautiful," I yelled from under the hemlock.

Clint looked up in surprise, seeing me for the first time. "Ahrr . . . that it was," he said. "Maybe this one should go to the taxidermist." With that he struggled ashore, carefully holding the trout safely enmeshed ahead of him.

We met on the iron bridge. I had to see that trout at all costs. And what a trout it was! I measured it with the handle of my landing net which had been scribed with nine, 12 and 15-inch marks. That trout measured 23 inches! And I thought of those other trout like two rows of cordwood in the dark water.

Clint removed the fly after probing for it, and I asked if I might see it. "That you may, lad," he said, smiling. "I'll autopsy this fellow and see what he was taking. I think it was the brown coddis." I took the fly. It was a slim, long but sparsely-hackled wetfly with a sliver of short wing on each side and a well-defined but thicker-than-usual brown body ribbed with embossed gold. The *hackle* was woodduck, the lemon shade preferred for the wing of the Gordon Quill and the Cahill. I studied the fly for a long time and noticed that the body followed the curvature of the hook, a Limerick.

"Aha!" Clint exclaimed, "It was a *coddis*," bearing hard on the British accent. And he showed me several he removed from the trout's stomach.

"That's what this is . . . isn't it?" I asked, holding up the fly.

"Right you are," he said. "I fish that fly here more than any other. If you notice, I tie mine a little more after the Irish style . . . the longer hackle, that is. You Americans tie hackle too short and too bushy for a good wetfly." I looked again and noticed how the few whisks of woodduck did extend beyond the end of the body, how the wings lay peculiarly on the sides of the fly, not above it, as did those of conventional dressing.

"I take it you tie," Clint said. I explained that I did, had a little shop and built a few rods. "Well, let me give you some then," he said.

For more than an hour, we talked patterns over open fly boxes, talked about the trout in Fishing Creek and fishing the wetfly. I thought I knew a little about the art and found out how little I really did know after listening to Clint. His dressing of the caddis intrigued me. Its curved body, short

A Night for the Caddis

wings and long, sparse hackle gave it a most-alive aura. It fairly seemed to twitch in repose.

"You can see I do not have many patterns," Clint said. " 'Tisn't necessary, even in your waters here." And, although they were filled, his boxes contained relatively few patterns. Instead, one box held a full range of sizes from 20 to four of one pattern, another box another pattern, etc. "The size and the shape of the tie count the most," he said. "On this stream give me the Woodduck and Brown and I'll take a trout. For a ten is the likes of your brown sedge, and a 12 the Grannom."

"You always fish the wetfly?" I asked.

He grinned. "Is there any other way! Even if you fish right in the surface, you're still fishing a wetfly. And that's where the trout feed; the big ones, just like today."

I copied the flies Clint gave me, especially those long-hackled, side-winged caddis pupae. At first I dressed them too fully hackled, finally settled down to no more than two turns of wooddduck, partridge or grouse. Some may have approached Clint's in appearance. "There's one more thing," he said. "Tie them in three weights. With a scissors cut fine strips from a toothpaste tube. Lay the strip once around on the hook for the mid-deep fly, twice around for the deep fly. And tie the high rider with na weight a'tall."

"How can you tell them apart," I asked.

"Easy," he said. "The color of the head. I finish the head of the deep fly with black silk, the mid-deep with brown and the high rider with yellow. If you do that, you'll have na trouble picking out the right one."

Clint was an instrument machinist specializing in precision prototypes and was on loan to a local firm. When he wasn't making instruments he was busy tying flies or driving along the Pennsylvania streams in his thundering old Bentley looking for new places to cast them. We fished together often during those two years he was in Pennsylvania, and I absorbed more about the caddis fly and about wetfly techniques from Clint than I could have from any dozen books. He did not know the scientific names for the many members of the caddisfly family. He knew the flies only by the fishermen's names. Yet his own lay terms for the larval forms were so elegant that others seemed expletive. "There are three kinds," he said. "Carpenters, weavers and masons. I call them that for the way they make their houses." We probed the riffles and backwaters to find them, and what revelations! We found the cemented cornucopia of the mason, the little wooden hut of the carpenter and the miraculous network of the weaver; whole colonies of larval forms whose life calendars were as regular as the time cycle of man.

"Now when these worms become pupae, you'll not have long to wait," he said. "You'll want to be astream then. Fish the deep fly but watch for flashes halfway down. And when the weather is hot, watch out! The pupae will be swimming up to molt along about dusk. The trout will be herding just under the top. Use your brown-bodied fly for the Grannom and the Brown Sedge, the orange body for the Cinnamon and the Speckled Sedge. And 't'wont hurt to have a bright green one for the Olive."

A Night for the Caddis

Clint peeled the little hut he held in his hand, to reveal a dull orange caddis worm. "Use this one all through May. It's the Cinnamon-Sedge. He lives in slow water, like this stretch. Fish him just under the top. The trout's na fool. It can get a pupa easier than the fluttering fly it's about to be. And it's the same with the mayfly. Get there when the nymph is struggling to the top. You'll fill your creel." Many times in past years I have been on the stream to see the water come alive with fish in unbelievable numbers rolling and bulging in pursuit of pupae or nymphs, the grist and mignon of the trout. Each time I see it, I itch a bit, feel goblins scamper in my belly and have to assume an almost monastic discipline just to tie the fly on the leader. I cannot outgrow it.

Clint was a patient teacher, even when I was first trying to emulate his roll casts with the light HEH double taper that had served so well. "It'll never work, Eddie, ma boy," he said. "Get an HCH and cut off three feet of the tip . . . then see what happens." I did, and thereafter the roll cast in tight spots was easy. I could switch out a repeat cast with a slight side-arm movement that even delighted Clint. But his patience waned when, time after time, I would not wait that split second before tightening against a trout that had mounted the fly. "Ahrr . . . that's when you lose them," he would say. "There's na hurry . . . mostly they hook themselves, if you'll only let them. You've been fishing the dryfly too long. Pull too soon, the fly slips away 'tween their lips and all you see is the flash of a trout you'll not catch for awhile."

Clint always contended the well-informed wetfly man

will take a trout from under the very nose of the dryfly man. For fishing the wetfly successfully calls for technique and stream lore that many an accomplished dryfly angler will not concede because he may not recognize their importance. Flipping the dryfly to stand stilt-legged behind a boulder or to bounce on top of a rip is one thing, and it takes ability to get it there. But once the fly alights, everything thereafter depends on its ability to float. There is little the angler can do from that moment except maybe give the fly a twitch. It will simply stay on top until it disappears in the mouth of a trout, sinks, skids away from drag or passes beyond the trout's lie to be whisked up and cast again.

Not so the wetfly, if it is artfully fished. Soon as it strikes the water and feels the current, its work begins. In its wet configuration, which the fly tier would do well to keep in mind, the wetfly assumes an entirely different posture, at once becoming scrutinized by the trout for size, shape, movement and stream depth like no dryfly ever was. And, instead of fishing for just a few seconds, it may undergo a duty cycle of two minutes or more, depending upon the knowledge of the man with the rod.

I know of one instance when a chap put his rod in the crook of his arm in order to load his pipe. By the time he had packed it, put back his tobacco pouch, found his lighter among the leaders in his shirt pocket and lighted his pipe, his cast, which had been dangling in the near side of a riffle, became taut from a 15-inch trout that had sucked down his caddis fly. He was a most surprised fisherman when he netted the trout. I wasn't, because that

A Night for the Caddis

incident was not so much the matter of luck that it appeared. That fellow was actually *fishing* the wetfly, whether or not he knew it. Keeping the fly in the water was another point Clint drummed into my head. "Are you fishing for trout, or are you casting for birds?" he would ask when I had become too aerial minded with needless casts. "They're down here!" And he would point toward the water. It was such a simple point to make, one that I recall everytime I see a fisher flailing away as if he were trying to burn holes in the air.

The last day we fished Clint beat me by only one trout. By then I had acquired the sense for waiting that split second before setting the hook and had not missed a rise. "You've the touch now," he enthused. "Another five years and you'll be as good as the best."

"How about as good as you?" I asked.

Clint laughed. "Check with me then. Come to Canada. When you're old you'll have na fishing worth a damn anyhow unless you vote in a ministry that will protect what you have now." Forty years later his remark has a clarion ring.

Before I had met Clint I probably was bent on having every pattern of fly there was. Fishing just two years with him changed that course. "There's only so much you can do to a fly," he said. "Do too much and you spoil it. Have too many and you're lost . . . like a hound trying to choose between a sausage and a weiner." How right he was.

There is really no need to have a so-called imitation for every insect known to hatch in any given stream. It would be sheer folly to attempt to tie or purchase the quantity needed, let alone tote it astream. Fortunately a single pattern of fly in a few sizes makes crossing between the orders of insects logical and possible. The Light Cahill in size ten, for example, doubles for some of the caddis pupae. And a size eight Stonefly works well when the larger mayfly nymphs are active. The March Brown is a good example of a pattern that ably represents more than one life form: the rising dun of a mayfly that has just shucked its nymphal case *underwater* (rare among mayflies); the pupa of the brown caddis; the nymph of the stonefly. But who needs to be told of the values of the March Brown! If there is a point to make, it is simply that one does not put away his March Browns when the hatch is over in the spring.

And many of the older patterns now considered fictions from the fly-maker's bench really have merits that all too frequently pass unnoticed. Early dressings such as the partridge, woodcock and grouse-hackled flies with gold-ribbed dubbing bodies were styled after the caddis in one of its many sizes and kinds. Whole series of patterns were developed around the caddis. They did well as sedges of their time. Even today the Queen of the Waters in sizes ten and 12, fished wet upstream is no slouch when the speckled sedge and the cinnamon sedge are paddling to the surface. As for the woodduck-hackled, brown-bodied caddis pupa Clint introduced me to, I have never been without it.

The afternoon that Clint left to return to Canada, we sat on the big running board of his Bentley. "There'll be a rise

A Night for the Caddis

along about dusk," he said. "Better fish it. It'll be a night for the caddis."

"I intend to," I said.

Clint put his gear in the back of the car, "dashed" the top and started the big engine. He waved and left, gunning the Bentley in first gear up the grade toward the blacktop leading to the highway. I heard the engine bellow between shifts then fade as the old car sped away. I never saw Clint again.

I waited an hour or two before walking below the old iron bridge along the opposite side of the bank that was shrouded by the hemlock. I slipped into the dark waist-deep water.

I held my rod at the ready and had several loops of line in my left hand, waiting to roll out the woodduck-hackled Brown Sedge upstream of a feeding trout. And if a trout would take the fly, I knew I could wait just that split second before tightening up. "Ahrrr . . . that's when you lose them," I thought.

I smiled as I waited for the first rise.

Pickerel: Wolf in Fish's Clothing

To extol the pickerel may seem off center and a bit strained these days, for the pickerel certainly is not the most beloved and sought after of all the fishes. It does have qualities, however, that set it apart as a truly vicious game fish, and it was a *big* pickerel that was responsible for making me a career fisherman before I was twenty. Again, the term, career fisherman, may not mean much either by the standards of worldly achievement. Yet, catching that long-billed ugly was so memorable that it triggered something in me almost metamorphic: stalking big pickerel. I have not outlived it, nor do I want to.

It all began in the mountains of Pennsylvania at Hunter's Lake, long known for its pickerel. Those who frequented Hunter's were the traditional livebaiters and trollers working the open waters off the points of marsh. The livebaiters fished with fat pond shiners and the

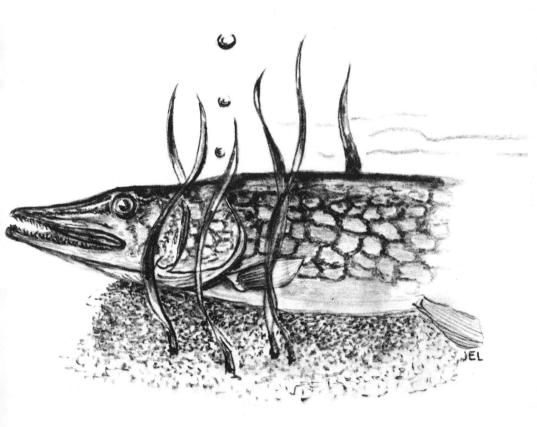

69 . . .

trollers dragged Skinner's and 4-Brothers fluted spoons tipped with treble hooks plumed in red, white, yellow and guinea-hen feathers. And they caught pickerel, plenty of them. Seldom, however, did anyone boat a fish "two-foot" long.

Still in my teens and with all the wisdom one acquires after a few years of flyrodding for trout, plugging for bass and trolling for walleyes, plus livebaiting and worming for the little delight makers that dwell in all ponds and lakes, I had a reasonably sound knowledge about fishing. Yet, I had never caught a large pickerel. But every time I experienced the zip-zip-zip of a small one that had latched on the shiner or leopard frog twitching the bobber, my hair bristled.

I soon learned that the *big* pickerel is a lone wolf, one to be *hunted* rather than just fished for, a true ugly with the disposition to match his wicked eye and teeth. I learned this from the man at Hunter's who ran the boat landing and collected the dollar for camping space. He had nailed several pickerel heads, ugly as gargoyles, to the trees near the landing, as evidence of what every pickerel fisherman could expect to catch. When I heard he claimed to have caught all of those outsized pickerel, I asked him how he could and others could not.

"Easy," he said. " 'Cept when they're teethin'. Just use big rigs and cast to places other people don't. 'Taint no use fishin' open water with them little wigglers folks are usin' when they ain't trollin'. 'Cause that ain't where the pickril is, and that's what they don't want. Ya hafta fish up in tha notches 'tween tha logs—right up inta tha bank with

Pickerel: Wolf in Fish's Clothing

sumthin' big. Not many's gonna do that. They're afeared of gittin' snagged. Oh, ya'll git caught all right—bound to—and ya'll lose more'n ya ketch." Then he grinned. "But how else ya gonna find out where they're at? If ya miss a big one, try fer it next week. It takes about that long fer him to git over his sulk."

Enthused with the lore, I contrived a "big rig." Even then I fiddled with lures and such, never being quite satisfied with the way other people made them. What I did to their inventions with a screwdriver, pliers and wire cutters should have been more than adequate cause for the big-name lure makers to offer handsome bounties for my hide. Using phosphor-bronze wire, I linked *two* number 4 spoons together (if one spinner would work, two would work better), tipping the contraption with a pair of double hooks, one trailing three inches behind the other. Including the two porkrind strips that were to be fastened on the following morning, the overall length of that rig must have been nine inches!

Shortly after daybreak the next day, the crank of the old knuckle buster was whirring, the spinners flopping and the porkrind fluttering. The gentle breeze that comes with sunrise was a perfect silent oarsman, inching the boat just a casting distance from the boggy shore.

In time a notch, heavily weeded on one side and flanked on the other by an old deadhead, appeared. The opening was no wider than the length of a yardstick. Normally I would have cast to the front of the notch, but remembering the boatkeeper's words, I let fly, expecting the "big rig" to drop midway up the notch. The knuckle buster whirred beautifully but the cast overshot and the spinners and porkrind splattered into the carpet of lily pads then disappeared.

From the very edge of the bog, six feet from where the big lure dropped, a huge dark shape darted, parting the weeds and the pads with one clean stroke, and for a moment I had the strange reaction that the rig should get out of there fast. But there was no chance. In a micro-second the spinners and porkrind were snatched from sight.

I struck hard but there was no need to; the pickerel turned broadside, as pickerel do when they strike, showing its green back and bronze side. It seemed as big as the blade of an oar. Fortunately, it shot out of the notch and into the lake proper. Had it turned back towards the bog, I should not be writing what follows.

That pickerel leaped like a salmon, bored like a small-mouth hooked on a crawdad and, like most pickerel, changed its direction with the reputed swiftness of a flying saucer. Getting it aboard posed a rather nasty problem. I had left the landing net at camp. And trusting that leg-long pickerel, which it later proved to be, to a heave on the line over the side and into the boat was unthinkable. The single hook holding it had worn a slot clear to the cartilaginous rim of the upper mandible. What had to be done had to be done in seconds.

Today I am not sure I would have done it. But, again, under the same circumstances, maybe I would. Since that day I have relived the experience many times, and each time I shudder at the thought.

Disregarding the obvious consequences, I stuck my

Pickerel: Wolf in Fish's Clothing

thumb between the pickerel's jaws, at the same instant managing to dig two fingers into its gill rakers. The pickerel landed in the boat, but I still do not know how my thumb came out of its jaws or how those two fingers cleared the gill rakers. I do know that my hand was a swollen salad of chopped fingers and pickerel teeth for many days. And to this day I believe the pickerel snarled at me.

Leg-long was no exaggeration. It was exactly as long as my leg, 30 inches. That is a big pickerel by any standard. Had it not been for the unmistakable chain markings and the absence of light, bean-shaped spots, I could have mistaken it for a pike which was unknown in that region at the time. It was a perfect specimen of *Esox reticulatus* except, perhaps, for the missing needle-like teeth I kept finding in my thumb and palm. And the fish did win a prize in the old *Hunting and Fishing* magazine contest that year, 1935. I received a level-wind reel that replaced the old knuckle buster and a three-piece tubular steel casting rod.

I have had a strange fascination for pickerel ever since. Few anglers, I have found, share such feelings, preferring to call it "snake" and other demeaning names. Of course, yearlings no bigger around than your thumb will snatch your streamers and probably make you hopping mad for it, especially if you are after bass. So will a five-inch trout take your fly and a seven-inch smallmouth hit your spinner, but you would hardly disqualify such fry as being "nuisance fish." The chances are you would, if the fish were a pickerel.

I believe the reason for the disinterest in the pickerel as a game fish is the result of ignorance about it and maybe a little snobbery. Fishermen are creatures of strange notion about the fish they catch. It was not so many years ago that the smallmouth was despised by trout fishermen only because it was indiscriminately planted in every creek, ditch or sump large enough to support the fish. And the Pacific bonito, until a few years ago, likewise was disqualified as a game fish and disliked by yellowtail anglers until its real fighting qualities were appreciated. Oddly enough, this was just after the yellowtail ceased to show for a few years. Then the "bonehead" came into its own.

The *big* adult pickerel is a predacious, savage loner, as difficult to catch as it is to find. Since that day at Hunter's I have caught hundreds in many places and hooked a few that may have been larger than the one that made me a career pickerel fisherman, and I do not pose here to be expert. I do believe, however, that I know why so few anglers ever hook, let alone net, a really big pickerel. A big one is so canny that it may live its lifetime without ever being detected! Most fishermen will not fish where the big one lurks. Had that one cast at Hunter's dropped where it was intended, instead of where it did—up close to the boggy shoreline—the 30-incher may have died a natural death. Few casters; fly, plug or spin, live so dangerously as to drop their lures (even the weedless ones) against the very shoreline to which fortune, that morning, took mine.

Once a pickerel has established its den (and each *big* pickerel has one) nothing short of a severe drop in water

Pickerel: Wolf in Fish's Clothing

level will cause it to vacate that den. The den affords seclusion and the access to the passing frogs, small snakes, birds and other fish that the pickerel can stuff into its gullet. Like an ornery tomcat under a bush waiting for a fat robin to come closer, the pickerel will lurk obscured against the edge of its haunt until the victim appears within range. Then, with the unbelievable speed and ferocity of its kind, it will strike its quarry into eternity.

As an illustration of the pickerel's voraciousness, I once witnessed the near demise of a small muskrat. I was fishing the Chicamacomico river on the eastern shore of Maryland. The small muskrat had been swimming across a narrow but deep gut nearly hidden by grass. Just as the muskrat approached the bank, a monstrous pickerel, skulking at the edge of the grass below the muskrat's port of entry, slashed at the little fellow, somehow missing it. How it missed I will never know, for its jaws seemed as large as an open cigar box. Unless that muskrat changed its way of life shortly thereafter, the pickerel surely got it in time.

I mentally marked the spot and later raised that pickerel twice and hooked it once during the following five seasons. It probably is still there unless a far wiser pickerel hunter than most sailed his lure into that gut where "no sensible" angler would fish. For there isn't one of 500 who would attempt to cast to that spot.

One hot July afternoon my Dad and I were wind drifting a lake in upstate New York for walleyes. In those days, a June Bug spinner with a long-shank hook draped with a big night crawler was potent for the walleye. If somebody hasn't written a new book, it still is. We had picked up three or four good walleyes and were drifting toward the landing, unaware that we were nearing a point of land faster than we should.

Dad's rod nodded twice and he struck. From the arch of the rod, the fish was small, probably not a keeper. When the leader knot cleared the water, we could see a yellow perch, perhaps nine-inches long, jerking behind the June Bug.

The unmistakable golden-green flash from the side of a huge pickerel suddenly eclipsed both the spinner and the perch. The rod tip swept low, and the line swished after the pickerel. Acting as quickly as one might be expected to under the circumstances, Dad free spooled as much line as the pickerel wanted. "Let's give him a few minutes," he said. "Maybe the hook is through the perch's mouth. It might catch." I drove an oar into the bottom to hold the boat. For long minutes the line did not move. Finally Dad struck hard. After two or three heavy surges the pickerel wallowed to the surface, threw the perch a country mile then streaked for places unknown. Undoubtedly, however, his destination was the place from which he had come—the den he had occupied for so many seasons.

Losing the pickerel is not the consideration here. The fact that a pickerel had wolfed down a fry-pan size yellow perch is.

By the time a pickerel has grown to outsized proportions, it has become most discriminating and avoids the metal and plastic gadgets fishermen throw its way (if they can get them there) as if it knew the name and catalog number of each one. An example follows.

Pickerel: Wolf in Fish's Clothing

One of the best places for pickerel I had ever found was a mill pond on the Eastern Shore. It was famous for its fishing for pickerel and largemouth bass and for the incident involving then Senator Harry S. Truman who fell tail over teacups into the pond. Until the dam was pushed out in 1972 by Hurricane Agnes, which lowered the water catastrophically, that pond yielded exceptional pickerel —although most anglers allowed on the water cast for largemouth which were equally exceptional. I fished it at every opportunity.

Several years ago I was on the pond going toward the upper end. The water was surprisingly clear, so clear that I was able to read the configuration of the bottom for the first time. What a revelation that was! Many of the suppositions I had made proved totally wrong. Places I had believed were shallow were deep. Areas which seemed they should be devoid of obstructions were filled with them.

I was headed for the haunt of a pickerel I had discovered three or four seasons before. The fish had struck my lures twice, but I had failed to boat it. The pond, then, had been its usually tawny dark color and the pickerel's lair was not visible (although I had contrived some solid pictures about it). As usual, I had landmarked the spot by sight of a fallen tree that sprawled at least 20 feet into the lake. The pickerel's haunt certainly was under that fallen tree!

This pickerel proved to have an almost psychic sense about knowing the difference between those things that had hooks and those that didn't. It was a big fish, and I was bent on boating it. The first time we had tangled the fish had stayed deep until near the end. Then, thrashing at the surface, it freed itself of the big spinner-bucktail rig. It had looked as broad as a shingle.

Realizing that the clarity of the water gave the pickerel the advantage, I used every caution and berthed the oars after making sure the drift of the boat was in line with what should be the pickerel's haunt. As the boat approached to within casting distance, I could see, for the first time, the end of an old stone wall which must have been laid before the dam had been built. It lay parallel to and about six feet from the tree. If ever there were an ideal place for a pickerel to hole up, this was.

The jointed plug dropped on target inches from the tree. After three feet of retrieve, old duckbill flashed from somewhere along the stone row—*not* from under the tree which I thought surely was his address—and I readied for the strike. It did not come. Instead, the pickerel swam parallel to the wriggling plug, but it kept a respectful distance away. I stopped reeling. The pickerel stopped. Then I eased the plug along until it was past the end of the stone row. Immediately the pickerel circled it several times, inspecting every aspect. Had the water been dark as usual, the entire act would have passed unnoticed!

The remainder of the retrieve was the same, except the pickerel widened the circles more erratically until the plug was about ten feet from the boat. Then the old wolf made a slashing sweep at the tip end of the plug without touching it and tailed for home. Undoubtedly a fly-size strip of porkrind fluttering from the tail hook would have brought a solid strike. That is not the point, however. The selectivity of the pickerel is.

Pickerel: Wolf in Fish's Clothing

The following year an enormous tandem-hook streamer, at least six-inches long, held that same fish for ten minutes until the pickerel finally doubled back around an underwater branch of the tree. To the best of my knowledge that pickerel is still there—provided it did not die when the water turned so foul after Agnes pushed out the dam. If still alive, it probably weighs seven pounds.

I have seen pickerel shadow the flight of little swamp birds flitting from stump to grass hummock and back —and catch them. I have watched aghast at the sight of a big one spearing a water snake. But this is the nature of the fish, and it is probably the reason for my liking to hunt it.

The pickerel has an unbelievable requirement for food. Even as far back as 1902 the Forest, Fish and Game Commission, State of New York, stated in its seventh annual report that two pickerel measuring five inches in length, under study, consumed more than 100 minnows in one day. So the pursuit by a leg-long oldster for a muskrat, bird, water snake or other hapless critter should not be surprising. But it certainly discounts the feasibility of using two-inch long wrigglers, if you are interested in stalking a big one.

My wife, Page, and I are scheduled for a week in Maine the last of this month for landlocked salmon and trout. I have reserved one full day, with a good guide, to stalk a couple of pickerel, and although I will settle for knicker length, I have my gear tuned for at least one as long as my leg.

I'll have my landing net. That's for damn sure!

Episode at Blackbeard's Hole

Although the rim of the sun was still minutes away, the morning was clear, and the air was clean, laden with the thick scent of the tide and spiced with the tang of the salt grass.

This was big country; the biggest, quietest place I had ever experienced. It was really the end of the world, it seemed. The marsh extended as far as the eye could see and appeared as vast as the sea itself. One might wonder where time and space began, if not here. I could have hidden behind an acorn.

For days I had scouted several of the accessible estuaries from the old wooden bridges which haphazardly connected the dirt and tar-patched roads which forever seemed to lose themselves in the labyrinths of the marsh. The particular crooked road on which I was now driving ended at the edge of a rotted dock.

As I set up my flyrod, the "pug-pug-pug" of a little boat engine sounded over the marsh. It was a cheerful sound, unnatural in a sense, yet somehow belonging to the scene, and I scanned the mouth of the wide river for the sight of the bull-pine skiff certain to appear. Years before I had caught my first "trout" from such a skiff by letting out pieces of peeler crab with the turn of the tide, and I had come to appreciate those heavy little skiffs powered with hardware-store engines. They were able fishers and could hold their course against tide or wind, could squeeze in close along the dropoffs denied larger boats.

The skiff appeared slowly from the mouth of the canal-like creek. For long moments it pressed against the deceivingly strong tide, making so little headway that, for a time, it seemed to stand still. Then I could see that the fisherman was an old man, for his hair was thick and white. Standing, he had waited until the skiff was in line with a point of marsh. He then dropped the grapple he had for an anchor over the side, palming out line that, swept by the tide, angled away from the bottom. Finally the grapple caught and held. The skiff snugged up short and nosed down sharply from the thrust of the tide. The old man leaned forward, pressing the spark plug shunt, and the engine stopped.

Soon he chucked over the side a heavy sinker followed by two trailing pieces of bait showing wet and white in the early light—doubtless peeler crab covering the business end of the snelled hooks. He set his rod against the washboard and waited.

A bony brown gull nestled on the water lifted into the air, arousing the other white gulls squatting on the sod-

Episode at Blackbeard's Hole

den, black spiles of the ancient dock. At its "Herka! Herka! Herka!" the white gulls soared over the place where the old man had cast. One, more curious than the others, swept low; then they all returned to their spiles to face in the same direction again.

In time the old man reached for his rod, hesitated briefly then struck hard. Working fast, he brought the fish to the surface where it attempted a last effort to break free. With a practiced sweep the old man lifted it clear of the washboard and into the skiff. The weakfish thumped against the floor boards. Then all was quiet.

He caught four or five good weaks before the sun had lifted above the sea. I knew he must have been aware of me wading along the spiles where the seagulls had squatted. Several times I had thrashed about, reaching from spile to spile, for the tide was strong as the flow of a salmon river.

One good weak had taken the streamer, its three pounds feeling like ten. And when I slipped it into the mesh bag, I knew why the eastern shoremen called weakfish "trout." Its sides, splashed with vignettes of gold and greenish-blue had shone like crushed, wet gems in the morning light.

The spiles, now like soggy, black yardsticks, measured the drop of the tide. The pull had lessened, and I ventured out toward a muskrat mound. The gulls had left the spiles and were circling and dipping over a patch of tuckahoe caught in the whorl of an eddy.

The old man's voice surprised me, "Ye caught one, I see. Looked like a good un."

"Nice trout I said.

"They's a better place, long about now, south a bit. I've got time—if you have. Wanna try?"

"Yes," I said. And with that the old man pulled on the grapple which held until the skiff had moved half the length of the line. It broke free then and in a moment landed with a thud in the skiff. The old man bent over to start the engine, and on the second pull it caught. He pointed the skiff toward the marshy point where I stood. As it drew alongside, I tossed the trout in the mesh bag into the skiff, handed my rod to the old man and climbed aboard. He pushed the throttle and turned the skiff toward the south.

"Name's Ira," he said above the "pug-pug-pug" of the engine. I told him mine and he nodded. "I allus finish up yonder," he said. "Gen'lly ketch a rock er two . . . times right fer it, certain."

He coaxed a little more from the engine and for at least ten minutes we sat silently, Ira peering ahead, his hand on the upright tiller which pivoted on a lag screw anchored in the oak chine. The years of sea and sun lay deep in the creases of Ira's brick-colored skin, and his arms showed the knots of muscle that, peculiar to old men, become more pronounced with the loss of tissue beneath the thinning skin. But his ice-blue eyes were ageless and seemed to see everything without pausing on a single object.

Except for the fragments of cut-up peeler on his bait board, Ira's skiff was clean and trim. Everything was chalk white. The tiller line that went all around the inside of the skiff was safely fastened by strong eye screws at

Episode at Blackbeard's Hole

every oak rib. A string mop hung from loops tacked to the stern thwart and the third rib.

Ira throttled to a slow idle after we had passed a sand spit, then turned into the mouth of a wide creek. After awhile he said: "We'll drift here," and he cut the engine. "You go ahead and switch that rod a'yourn. I'll watch a bit and tend to these fish. Here hand me your trout." He glanced toward the edge of the marsh. "Tide's a long way from slack yet and they's a good chance a rock might like that feather ye got thar." And he studied the streamer. "Kinda like the color of a peeler claw, ain't it. Looks right good!"

While Ira cleaned his five trout and my one, I cast the streamer to the spots he pointed out. But I was more interested in watching Ira's skill with his knife. With a quick stroke from vent to tongue, he opened each weak, then removed the entrails and gills with a single movement. He cleaned the six fish in moments. Then he leaned over the side and washed his hands.

The weaks were alike as matches in a box. Their orange maws and fins were still bright; but the gem-like brightness of their sides had gone. "Them's purty fish," Ira said. "Nuthin' I ever seed's any purtier . . . less'n it's a. . ."

The rod was nearly wrenched from my grasp. There was no need to strike. And I turned to see the last of the huge boil and the flash of a striper.

"God A'mighty," Ira hollered. "That's a good un. Hang onta it. We'll folly it iffen we hafta," and he reached for the paddle hanging under the gunwale. "It's one a them cows! Stay with it. Bigger'n legal—but we'll take care a that." He stroked with the paddle, turning the skiff toward the bigger water where the striper was headed.

The striper, not too sure it was in trouble, ran in short but heavy thrusts, sampling the annoyance in its jaw. And despite its long history with bass, landlocks, weaks, even muskies and other stripers, the rod felt like a toy. But the leader was stout, giving a little edge for bearing hard if I had to. From those first surges I knew I would—and I had doubts.

When I glanced at the reel I was surprised that so much line had slipped away. Then the striper ran hard. The 100 feet of casting line, as I had feared, soon were gone. The first of the backing quickly slipped through the rod tip and the line splice darted underwater. Ira's strokes were strong, the bow lifting with each sweep. "God A'mighty," he puffed. "Ain't seen one like this un in yars. Hang on . . . I'll hep ya. It's a big un, fer certain."

The striper now was in the deeper water at the mouth of the creek, no longer doubting that it was in trouble. It had reverted to its innate knowledge that prying and wedging against the irregular bottom should free it of the hook. The thump from its jaws bumping the bottom telegraphed clear to the reel seat, and I wondered how many times this one had been hooked before, how often it had nursed the sore spot where a hook, buried deep in the cartilage of its jaws, had not rusted away.

The line slackened a little, then cut through the water, quartering against the tide. "It's off that thar shelf. They's a hole thar yonder where Blackbeard's supposed ta hid his treasure chest," Ira hollered. "It's 90 honest feet . . . they plumbed it."

Episode at Blackbeard's Hole

The backing continued to slip away. Then all movement ceased. I arched the rod clear through the grip, even rapped against it to set the fish in motion. Ira saw this and said: "We'll go out yonder. Keep tight till we're on t'other side." The bow of the skiff lifted in pulse with his paddle strokes.

As the line described a curve on the outer side of where the striper had holed up, Ira said, "Give it a nudge or two. From 'ere ye might fetch 'im loose." I did, and it worked! The striper reversed its path to run toward the very place it had taken the streamer. As it rose to go into shallower water, the line slackened again. Ira swung his paddle to the other side of the skiff and turned in pursuit.

I retrieved line in arm lengths and thought I saw the line splice. But even when bearing hard against the tide, the striper moved like it had just been hooked, easily reclaiming whatever line I had hopefully gained.

The backing now was thinned to the point where the hub was only moments away. With the seventh sense of a man who knows big fish, Ira cranked the engine and tillered the skiff to follow the striper now headed for the mouth of the creek, and I gained a few yards of line again, meanwhile looking for the line splice once more.

When the rod relaxed for a moment, I sensed trouble. Either the striper was reversing direction, or it was about to surface. I stripped in line fast. This might be the end. It had been all of 15 minutes since the hook up, and the striper was still having it all his way. Then, very easily, it wallowed along the edge of the marsh, and we could see its length for the first time. It was longer than a yardstick. Ira pressed the throttle and the skiff plowed ahead. "I'm goin' toward the creek to head 'im off," he yelled. "If it gits up thar, it'll git inta them damn net stakes fer certain."

The rod bowed hard under the load, and then I let back, hoping the striper would head out toward the deeper water again, instead of up the creek. And it did—with a surge that all but splintered the rod butt. The backing cut sharply into my hand. Fumbling for my handkerchief, I called to Ira to turn about.

The skiff swung in time to prevent all of the backing from slipping away, but the striper did not stop. Ira opened the throttle and the skiff followed the slice of the line through the water and out beyond the mouth of the creek. Gradually the angle of the line increased. The striper was down deep now ... probably as deep as Blackbeard's treasure chest. Ira slowed the engine to an idle, and we drifted toward the big water.

"He's fought ye right smart," Ira said. "Prolly wearyin' a little by now, I reckon."

I kept the strain on the striper as we drifted, letting the backing run out slowly, while the skiff passed over the fish. There was no movement. It had sounded. "Let's try circlin' round it," Ira said. "Got enough line? I'll cut 'er sharp. Cain't let it rest. Ye gotta keep it moving."

I looked at the remaining backing. "Do it," I agreed. And Ira started the skiff into a tight starboard turn, throttling up when the bow felt the tide. More backing slipped away when the angle changed, and the line hummed into a deep curve against the pull of the tide.

We made a complete circle. There still was no movement from down deep in Blackbeard's hole. "How much pull will that gear a yourn stand?" Ira asked. And I told him it would hold so long as the striper did not run out all of the backing. "Let's circle again, then," he said.

At half circle, the next time around, I felt a quick surge. Ira saw the rod tip jerk and quickly changed course again to follow the slice of the line. The striper was coming up. And as it bulled toward the surface, I stripped in line, knowing that whatever was about to happen very probably would be the climax.

"Watch out," Ira yelled. "They're great for comin' ta tha top and rollin' in tha line, t'wards tha end."

The striper broke, not 50 feet from the bow. Its tail was as big as a broom. Then it bored for the open bay. Ira brought the little engine up to everything it had, but the striper continued toward the big water. When the backing was down to the very hub, I checked the speed of the skiff against the determination of the striper and brought the rod up hard in one last effort to turn it. It never stopped. In its final thrust for life, the striper outraced full throttle and was beyond any restraints.

The backing snapped into the air, trailing like a kite string, then fell to the surface and disappeared. We drifted quietly. I dabbed at the crease in the palm of my hand with the red-stained handkerchief.

"That was a fish," Ira said. "That really was a fish." He reached into a crab basket, unwrapped a towel, and handed me a bottle of the smokiest, brownest whiskey I had ever seen. "Here, pour some inta that cut," he said, "and pour some inta ya'self." The label was mimeographed.

I removed the handkerchief and poured the whiskey into the cut. It burned. And my throat burned after two swallows. I handed the bottle back to Ira and he took a long draught. " 'Tweren't no fault a yourn," he said. "That rock jest warn't about to be ketched today, that's all. Doubt ya coulda done any better even with my heavy gear. Once they git goin' straight line like that, they ain't ta stop very easy." I looked at Ira's stiff, old boat rig with the reel spooled with thick cuttyhunk and the brake set up to the point of no return. That was quite a concession.

For awhile we drifted with the tide. I looked once more toward the place where we last saw the backing and hoped that somehow the striper would free itself of the hook and those hundreds of feet of trailing line.

Ira wrapped the towel around his bottle of whiskey and put it in the crab basket. Then he squinted at the position of the sun. "Hafta tend ta crab pots t'day," he said. "And I hafta cut up eels fer bait. 'Sides, the tide's gittin' flat anyhow." So he pulled on the engine and headed back toward the old dock where we had met. I leaned against the bow plate and watched the edge of the marsh, now sandy brown below the roots of the grass, go by.

In time, Ira cut the engine and the skiff mushed into the muck below the spiles. "You keep my trout," I said. "I'm staying in town and have no place to fix it."

Ira nodded. Then he looked toward me, his ice-blue eyes seeing nothing and everything. "Comin' by these parts agin' soon, mebbe?" he asked.

"Not for awhile," I said.

"You're a soldier shippin' out soon," he said. I told him I

Episode at Blackbeard's Hole

was. "So was I . . . first war, that is." Then he squinted. "Mebee it's good ya came fishin' down 'ere after all. We uns have a sort of sayin' 'round these parts that iffen you've been here b'fore, ya allus come back—least one time." He paused. "We'll fish another day . . . you watch. We uns down 'ere know things . . . don't hafta be told. We jest know. And that's fer certain."

I gathered my gear and reached for Ira's hand. It was hard and bony. Then Ira pointed toward a far point of marsh. "My hoose is jest a piece to tha left at the end of tha fork ya'll come ta goin' back," he said. "When you're back, jest drive up. I'll be thar—lessen I'm crabbin' or fishin' —and that's most of the time."

With that Ira paddled the skiff inho the deeper water. Then he soaked the string mop overboard and swabbed the inside of the skiff. After wringing it damp, he hung it in place below the gunwale. He cranked the engine, it's "pug-pug-pug" fading into the distance.

"Take care, ya hear!" he called.

The seagulls were returning to wait for whatever the new tide, still hours away might bring. I sloshed through the high grass and noticed how tall the soggy spiles were. The gulls would wait a long time, I thought.

Soon Ira, silhouette of a breed apart, and his little skiff were rounding that point of marsh from where he had come. As I watched him pass from sight, I wondered about ever fishing with him again, like he said.

But, like some of the folk lore of the eastern shore that I later learned; much of it couched in a mysticism that in time becomes so curiously acceptable, if not believable,

Ira's adage about "allus comin' back—least one time" did prove prophetic. For on a hot June day, two years later, I was driving down the weeded lane at the end of the fork that led to Ira's "hoose", to find him rigging a crab line.

As he turned from his task, at the sound of my steps, he studied me for a moment. Then, apparently not at all surprised that I was there, he greeted me with a huge grin. "See! I toldja," he said. "We uns down 'ere jest know things."

"That's for certain," I said. And for a moment no time had passed since that day we first met.

During the next few seasons that we fished Blackbeard's, the points of marsh and the mouths of the canal-like creeks, I learned something about the ways of the "rock" and the "trout" of the eastern shore. But I learned far more about the way of life of Ira, the waterman, who, although he could hardly read or write, lived as he chose, very probably like his father before him and perhaps his grandfather. His life was simple, I suppose, yet gut satisfying, for Ira lived wholly apart from the madding crowd.

Ira had no car because he needed none. He used his skiff to take his catches of crabs and fish to market and to haul back "boughten" staples and fuel. He took time from his crabbing and fishing to grow a few rows of corn and some tomatoes. He even painted his house once in awhile.

There were times when I may have envied him.

Ira still drank the same brown, smoky whiskey from the bottle with the mimeographed label. I never asked him where he got it. Occasionally his tippling made him slack-jawed, especially if he had had a good week of crabbing. And I expect he was not above poaching a bit. Several times I saw hanging from a post near his house wild ducks "curin'," as he said, long after legal season.

We never again hooked a "rock" with a tail big as a broom at Blackbeard's or anywhere else. Had Ira lived longer, we may have. But he died—possibly as he would have wanted it—in his little, white skiff not far from the deep hole where it was claimed Blackbeard had hidden his treasure chest.

I sometimes fish for "trout" on the turn of the tide where the old spiles were. Now there are crisp, new houses along the fork of the road, and the whine of outboards has replaced the "pug-pug-pug" of the little hardware-store engine. But the scar in my hand from where the line cut it that day we chased the big striper remains, a reminder of the episode at Blackbeard's Hole. And an episode it was; one that ended with a waterman's simple adage that strangely became a prophecy.

That's for certain.

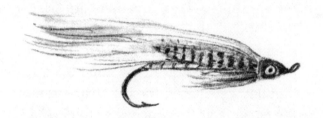

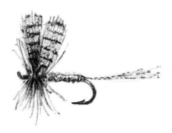

What Fly
Is That?

Having been a flyrodder for nearly 50 years, I feel qualified to say that, as a whole, flyrodders are a strange lot. My own antics and notions through the years will bear that out, because I know they must have seemed mighty peculiar to those of my family who are not flyrodders, perhaps more so to those who are not even fishermen or fisherwoman . . . with emphasis on the latter.

We too often quibble over infinite details while not showing the least amount of horse sense, or more appropriately, fish sense. We'll stand where fish feed and cast to where they do not—then bewail that the trout just are not on the rise or maybe were washed downstream during the big March flood. We'll cuss the leader for being too heavy or too limp, the hackle for being the wrong hue, or holler about the rod, the reel, the line for one reason or another, instead of admitting that we, ourselves, spooked the trout with shadows tall as a eucalyptus tree and with wading about as stealthy as a Marine platoon at double time.

The fly is most often blamed, however, and in search for the one that is faultless, the angler keeps adding to his inventory of super flies at a dollar per copy, hoping that the right one will cure all his ills. The exactness of pattern, the quest for the perfect bronze hackle, the sorting of lemon woodduck feathers for those few having the faintest of black tips, the counting of body segments when wrapping a quill; these are some of the values stressed by flyrodders who, not so many years ago, viewed with tongue in cheek similar idiosyncracies of British anglers as being just so much more stuff in the arcanum of tying flies. British flies were not suited to American waters; so said certain of our patriarchal flyrodders. Yet, the Scotch, Irish and English patterns caught a lot of American trout, salmon and bass—and do today—despite their soft hackle, too-long wings, fussy bodies and the like.

Trout and most gamefish can be exasperatingly selective, sometimes refusing at the last microsecond the best of this year's patterns so carefully fashioned on the best hooks made. Yet, one sometimes wonders why it is so difficult to explain why a feeding trout, observed to be gorging on little stoneflies, will refuse a good(?) representation of a stonefly and a moment later gulp down a strange gadget called Willard's Owl Hackle, the size of an unshelled peanut. It would be illogical to conclude that

What Fly Is That!

the stonefly pattern was not the right color, size or shape, because the trout preferred something in the mystique of Willard's contraption. Or maybe it just hated owls.

I have known able flyrodders who spoke of flies as "that little gray one" or "the long skinny, brown fly with the speckled wings" that were worth at best a few pennies. Yet, because they knew how to use their flies, those chaps outfished others who knew their Latin and Greek, entomology and ichthyology, and the contents of the latest, best catalogs listing impedimentae essential to the "man with the fly."

One time I was resting a pool, after having creeled a good brown, when a pleasant fellow emerged from the bushes to sit beside me. We exchanged thoughts and compared reasons for the few rises. He explained that the only fly to use on this creek in May was the Pine Creek Special. This was interesting because the creek was the Pine, one I had fished for over 20 years and knew well.

"What's a Pine Creek Special?" I asked. And he told me about woodduck wings, cream dubbing body, dun hackle. "It's the only pattern the trout will take now," he said.

I showed him the Hendrickson in the flykeeper. "That's it," he said. But after examining it more closely, he said, "Ah . . . there's the difference. The Pine Creek Special has a brown head, not the tannish color of the head on your fly." I learned later that he disregarded standard patterns, preferred only those developed locally by a fellow who really knew his hackles.

Is there an exact pattern, one so superior to others like it, for simulating a natural insect? The Light Cahill, a pattern long exhorted for its effectiveness, is tied and fished as dryfly, wetfly, nymph, even streamer. It fishes well. Yet, if you order one Light Cahill dryfly from each of six reputable suppliers and examine each fly carefully for authenticity (as the suppliers would have it, or you think it should be), you will probably conclude that the workmanship, materials and style are to your liking but that the flies differ in some respects. Actually, you will have a nice assortment of light-colored flies ranging from ivory through tan; having divided or slanted wings or natural pearl mallard (or mallard dyed to represent woodduck), real woodduck (with or without black-barred tips); and having hackle which ranges from pale cream to medium ginger, sparse or full; dressed close to the eye or set back for balance(?); on standard, 1X or 2X-long, regular or light-weight hooks. Still, each is a Light Cahill. Of course it is. If beauty is in the eye of the beholder, the accuracy of fly pattern justifiably is in the eye of the flymaker.

A color-blind fisherman may not differentiate between olive and gray; but this disability, if it can be so termed, makes him no less the productive fisherman, if he knows the real wrinkles of the game: where, when and how to place the fly.

Consider the neophyte who ordered Blue Duns from a catalog house and received Ginger Quills instead? The chances are he still caught trout, despite the error, until some knowledgeable fellow pointed out that he could not possibly have caught trout on a Ginger Quill when the Blue Duns were hatching, a condition which neither the neophyte nor the trout apparently knew. Then, too, there

What Fly Is That!

is the fisher who steadfastly flicks a Hendrickson, size 12, all season long and is consistent with it, and the angler with poor eyesight who struggles and squints to see the white wings of his Royal Coachman with which he takes a good share of fish every season. And what about the chap who says, "Just gimme an eight. I don't care about the pattern, long as it's an eight."

What fly is that? What fly do you use? These questions are repeatedly asked of successful anglers. Answers? Blue dun, size ten; Coachman—I dunno the size; Quill Gordon, size 12; Brown Bivisible, size 14—all I ever use; Gray Hackle-Orange, size ten, tied sparse; Twiddle-Wiffet, pale series number four, size 13, modified with plum hackle veiled with the anal fuzz from the Ethiopian sacred White Goink.

Was there a *best* fly? The Coachman had a reverse hackle. The others did not. The Brown Bivisible had an all-hackle body with a turn of white at the eye, but no wings. The Gray Hackle-Orange had the only gold-ribbed body but no tail whisks which it should have. And the Quill Gordon was the only fly with dun hackle and quill body. But the Twiddle-Wiffet, outstandingly different, snagged the largest trout and may be cause for triggering new onslaughts of the Ethiopian sacred White Goink by gimlet-eyed feather benders armed with scissors, tweezers and file boxes labeled G.

One hot June afternoon I had waded ashore at the tail of a slick, so I would not interfere with a flyrodder engrossed with combing the upper reach with the most beautiful casting I had seen in a long time. He laid out his line in storybook fashion, meticulous and crisp in every move-ment. Time after time he rested leader and line exquis-itely upon the surface of the hard-to-reach water in order to achieve the long, quiet drift so essential for interesting big browns.

What Fly Is That!

I appreciated that his fly was minuscule, for it left no rings. It seemed the smallest fly I could imagine. I had fished with 24's with debatable success and had doubts about hooks any smaller. The purpose of a hook, as I see it, is to hook, not tickle a fish. (And for this, I expect all kinds of repercussions from proponents of the 28's.)

Despite his artistry with rod and mini-size fly, the fisherman raised nothing. In time he withdrew to the stream's edge, reeling in line as he waded backwards. I approached and asked if he were using a small nymph. He nodded and reached for the end of the leader. That fly was small; so small that I could not see it. Nor could a trout. Even the fisherman could not see it. It wasn't there!

"It must have snapped off," he said. "I don't know how long ago." Then he added: "These 28's are hard to tie on well." He reached into his fishing vest, to take out a small plastic vial containing flies the size of spots on dice. "These are different from the tiny black midge," he said. "They're tied with special gossamer imported from Belgium. No other thread does the job. I buy these from a fellow in Missouri. He's the only flytier who uses it. And the fly acts better for it."

Maybe, just maybe, we have gone off the deep end with our hypotheses about flies. At best, artificial flies merely *represent* insects, spiders, crustaceans and minnows. Of itself, the hook, which is seldom concealed, rules out the possibility of imitation. An insect with a bronze appendage the size of a hook is a rarity, indeed.

A Pale Evening Dun with its body turned muddy gray from the effects of a floatant which brings out the color of a dark tying thread (wrongly used) is not a Pale Evening Dun. Yet, I have seen one which turned dark green raise trout with surprising success when the *Ephemerella Dorothea* was on the water. The angler using the green fly persisted he was using a Pale Evening Dun, however, and was oblivious to the chameleon-like quality of his fly.

A Royal Coachman with unwound peacock herl is not a Royal Coachman, but the imperfect fly is sometimes more effective. And a Ginger Quill without light and dark bands in the quill body is really not a Ginger Quill. Trout are seldom aware of the difference, I have found.

Sometimes an angler will boast of the number of trout he has caught with one particular fly so riddled as to be unidentifiable. But don't try to convince him that the fly is not the one with which he started! Therefore, I have become intrigued with some patterns which remain so sacrosanct that their production is limited, for want of urine-stained fur, fuzz from the scrotum of the ram and, soon perhaps, the hair from the ear of a dirty old man. It was Charles Cotton, early English fisher and writer who, when writing how to tie the Fiery Brown, said: "...the dubbing for which is to be had out of the skinner's lime pits, and of the hair of an abortive calf, of which the lime will turn to be so bright as to shine like gold."

He said further: "...then a brown that looks red in the hand and yellow betwixt your eye and the sun."

If still alive, Dan Cahill would be quick to say that the Light Cahill that is seen today is not the fly he devised of lemmon woodduck wings, brown hackle and rabbit fur body. What Rube Cross, Roy Steenrod, Theodore Gordon

What Fly Is That!

and William Chandler did with the original Cahill has certainly benefitted flyrodders. But what happened during the interim from the time of Dan Cahill's dark pattern to the time when the light pattern was developed? Surely Dan's pattern continued to take trout. The Light Cahill is as different from the Dark as the Iron Blue Dun is different from the Blue Quill. Yet, how many times have you known both Cahills to take trout from the same waters, under the same conditions, at the same time? You probably will say, many.

Years ago I determined to find out if the hue of the hackle on a dryfly is significant, and I undertook a study repeated over many seasons on waters I knew well. The stream contained both native brook trout and brown and rainbow trout, holdovers from previous stockings.

I tied in sizes 12, 14 and 16, two patterns, each abundant in season, effective and popular: the Quill Gordon and the Light Cahill. For the Gordon, I chose hackles ranging from near-white badger through iron-blue, for the Cahill, ivory through brown. Many of the hues were obtained by carefully dyeing natural white and ginger hackle. The flies were tied as closely the same as possible. Only the hue of the hackles differed. The wings were upright (sail type) slanted slightly rearward. The hackles were sparse and the bodies and tails were correctly proportioned.

I would fish the flies fairly and to best advantage (which I did)—the Gordon when the *Iron Fraudator* was on the water and the Cahill when the *Stenonema Ithaca* was. Leaders were nine-feet long, tapered to 4X points for the size 12 and 14 flies and to 6X for the size 16. The single foreseeable difficulty was the human frailty of self-discipline: changing to a darker or lighter hackled pattern each time I caught a trout!

The results of those years of testing with off-hue patterns verified the opinions I had reached long ago but could not have otherwise proved. I know they will be questioned, if not outright disputed. After all, some people like brown shoes and other do not. And just who is that bloke debunking all that the hackle hunters of America stand for!

I'll stick with the results which follow.

1) The hue of a hackle, if of the basic color, means little, so long as it is sparse and allows the body of the fly to rest on the surface.

2) Sparseness de-emphasizes the hue of hackle and emphasizes the hue and shape of the body and tails.

3) Shadows from darker hues may spook a rising trout.

4) A sparse 12 appears smaller than a thickly-hackled 14.

5) A sparse hackle allows the wings to show well (if wings are important!?).

6) Oversize hackle (even if it is webbed) trimmed to size is more lifelike than untrimmed hackle of standard gauge, and it floats the fly better.

7) Mixed grizzly and ginger are, perhaps, the most consistently effective hackles.

I do not pose these results as the panacea for dryflies (and dryfly fishermen). Too frequently conclusions are premature and biased, becoming what the tester wants them to be. And the most provocative discourse on fish habitudes, the wisest analysis of their psyches, the best catalog on flies ever printed is but the viewpoint of opportunistic flyrodders—guys like you and me—who have notions. And that takes us back to the first premise that flyrodders are a strange lot. For they often put the emphasis on the wrong syllable.

Having batteries of flyboxes filled with crisp, unused flies may be impressive. But having a fly box containing a few specific patterns in the sizes that satisfy "matching the hatch"—an illusion at best—is all the more impressive for its efficiency and economy. I have known some men who must take along an index to find a fly from somewhere among the lumps in their fishing vests. Generally, by the time they have found the fly they think will work, the rise will be over or some joker with a "long, skinny brown wetfly" that he has used all day will have creeled the fish they had hoped to raise.

At the risk of being chastised for over simplification, I list the dryfly patterns, hybrids all, which those years of testing and time to the present have convinced me will take trout whenever trout are feeding on the surface. These are not limited geographically. I take them everywhere I go, and I take them with confidence.

1. For brown-gray mixes including the Dark Cahill, Adams, Blue Dun, Whirling Blue Dun, March Brown, Hendrickson. Wings: barred teal. Hackle: sparse mixed

grizzly and brown. Body: muskrat or equivalent fur. Tails: mixed grizzly and brown. Sizes: 8, 12, 16.

2. For sandy-light gray mixes including Light Cahill, Little Marryat, Light Hendrickson, Light Stonefly. Wings: gray mallard. Hackle: sparse mixed ginger and salt-and-pepper (chinchilla) grizzly. Body: opossum or equivalent fur. Tails: mixed ginger and salt-and-pepper (chinchilla) grizzly. Sizes: 10, 14.

3. For sandy-light gray mixes with segmented body including Gray Quill, Cahill Quill, Ginger Quill, Quill Gordon. Wings: lemon woodduck or the tannish feathers from a mallard drake. Hackle: sparse mixed ginger and salt-and-pepper (chinchilla) grizzly. Body: quill from the coarse feathers of a duck or goose. Tails: mixed ginger and salt-and-pepper (chinchilla) grizzly. Sizes: 12, 16.

4. For bright-colored flies such as Cranefly, Queen of the Waters, Red Quill. Wings: barred teal. Hackle: sparse mixed brown and grizzly. Body: raffia dyed orange. Tails: mixed brown hackle and teal. Sizes: 8, 12.

5. For large terrestrials, grasshoppers and the like. Wings: brown bucktail tied flat. Hackle: grizzly tied palmer, underside trimmed flat. Body: straw raffia over kapok for floatation. Sizes: 4, 8.

6. For midges, gnats and tiny terrestrials. Wings: none.

Hackle: sparse badger, the black trimmed to leave only a speck of white. Body: black tying silk. Tails: same as hackle or sparse guinea. Size: 18 short shank or 20.

It is wise to be scientific about fishing, provided we recognize that any fish has a personality and will accept or reject a lure, artificial or genuine, purely by choice. This is true of trout, salmon, bass, stripers; even a catfish can be choosey, no matter how fine you cut the bait. But when it comes to dryflies, fewer patterns, perhaps the six hybrids outlined here, will serve you well, if you know how to serve them to the trout. When you have to ask yourself, "What fly is that?" or have to fumble through an index to identify it, you might try asking the trout, because only the trout knows.

Fly-Rodding
for Stripers

The cruisers, sailboats, floats, and moorings taking over our coastal rivers and estuaries have caused the majority of anglers to seek the open waters of the "beyond" to escape clutter and racket. The trollers have had to; the spin casters have preferred to. They contend they are seeking fish. I suspect they are seeking fishing space.

For the moored boats, even their moorings—those nemeses of fishing lines, leaders, lures, and a good disposition—can become a boon to the fly caster. When the tide has begun to flow, pointing the boats upstream, wakes and eddies form astern of the bobbing hulls and the wobbling floats where baitfish gather. Stripers are aware of these gathering places and, if they are at all affected by the presence of the boats and moorings, they are affected favorably. Each year they go about their usual business of ascending the same tidal rivers peppered with the stuff of the boating world.

The spin fisherman will shudder at the thought of his light monofilament amidst those bobbing moorings and barnacled bottoms. It's true; his 8- or 10-pound nylon is out of place in this environment.

But here the opportunistic fly caster is at home, provided he has suitable gear: a rod of sufficient length with the guts to "hold" clear to the butt; a level, unknotted leader of 20-pound nylon; a good reel spooled with at least 50 yards of backing under a torpedo-taper line; and streamers tied on hooks stout enough to survive striped bass. With such equipment any reasonably experienced fly caster can expect to take stripers of school size and larger from the eddies trailing those moorings and boats.

Like all striper fishermen, the fly fisherman will strike into bass he simply cannot hold, even with 20-pound nylon. An unpreventable double-back around a float line generally spells defeat. Moreover, stripers have not read the literature of the "fairy wand" cult, preferring to live by the rules of their own book. Stepped-down and knotted leaders have no place here, nor do 2-ounce rods, regardless of their label. Light tackle will yield nothing but a lost bass, especially if you must give him the butt and make things grunt.

I have struck bass so large they showed no reaction to a hard strike. Instead they merely tacked into the current with hardly a tail flap to run out the backing clear to the hub, despite the restraints of snugged-up reel and critically arched rod. So, if you are the fly fishermen given to the light touch obtained through many years of trouting, save yourself grief and look for stripers in water free of obstructions.

Night tides, stripers, and big streamers are synonymous. Water seemingly devoid of anything resembling a bass becomes marked at night with the bulges, *bops,* and *splats* of boldly feeding linesides which have moved from the channel bed to maraud in lesser waters for an hour or two. One of my preferred stretches is so thickly studded with moorings that many anglers would speculate fishing there is futile, that a bass of any intelligence would not be there in the first place and if it were, would get out fast. Not so! But let others so believe. I like to be alone sometimes, too.

There is a little blue sailboat moored just outside the channel dropoff. During the early running of the tide, it is just out of reach of my best casts. After the first hour, when 4 feet of sand show beneath the rock wall, I can inch along toward the channel and drop the streamer behind the rudder in a swirl from which, season after season, I have struck and beached . . . and lost . . . big stripers.

One hit the streamer after it and ricocheted off the transom. I had beached four good bass and was, perhaps, overconfident when this one struck. I strong-armed him with the hope that he would take to the air. He did, like a fresh-run silver salmon, in full-length profile, his body wetly reflecting the brightness of the moon. That sight was the fulfillment of the season. Esthetics, although not measured in pounds and inches, are frequently the most rewarding aspects of this sport.

Experts have long conjectured as to why striped bass will push their way through a school of silversides to smash a streamer. "Why," they ask, "will a bass chase something no thicker than a pencil, when bait fish twice or three times that size are everywhere in pods or schools?"

The answer may remain forever with the bass. To hazard a guess, I think it may be because the streamer does what you make it do and therefore does not match the movement, the speed, the direction of the schooled baitfish, which follow a unified pattern of direction, activity, and depth. It may suggest, then, a cripple which has departed the pattern of the school. If so, a law of survival—that cripples be killed off first—may apply. Or the streamer, being different, may represent a predator savory to the bass. Only the striper really knows. The point here is, regardless of the reasons, a 3- or 4-inch streamer is large enough and enticing enough to make stripers strike —stripers that will test you and your tackle to the limits.

There are times when a striper will obligingly "repeat rise" if you quickly cast your streamer a few feet ahead of the spot where it last boiled. Allowing for the speed of the tide, try to have the streamer in motion at least 4 feet in front of the bass. You can be ready to make a rising fish "repeat" by false-casting a comfortable length of line over the area where it has been surfacing. When it next rises, quickly drop the streamers upstream of its wake and prepare for the strike. Invariably the bass will take it solidly, unless he is feeding on grass shrimp. But that's another story.

Fly-Rodding for Stripers

With all the streamer patterns available today, my log still shows that three patterns, tied on both long and short hooks, have accounted for all the stripers I have caught during the past many seasons. And I sometimes believe just one of the three would have done as well. The long and short-shank hooks are an important consideration. Given the choice of two streamers, I would select any one of the three patterns—one tied on a short shank, the other on a long.

One night about two hours before dawn I had been raising bass with regularity that was annoying because they were striking tormentingly short. Efforts to vary retrieve and change the situation were futile. The streamer was a 6X long shank, which I preferred for the glinting, long-body effect.

Then I recalled one of Hal Gibbs' contentions: "Stripers hit the head of a baitfish, and don't ever doubt it." Hal's Gibbs' Striper was built accordingly. The hook was a short-shank, round bend, size 1. And it had to be hand-honed to a point approximating that of a needle.

I waded ashore to explore the boxes in my fishing jacket for a streamer similar to the one I was using but tied on a short or regular-length hook. A tandem salmon streamer, from which I clipped the connecting monofilament and tail hook, seemed the answer. Double-knotting it, I let fly.

The next sentence should read that the short strikes became hard, solid strikes. And they did. Three chunky stripers taken on the short-shank streamer from the same water which previously had yielded nothing but misses seemed to prove something. Though the jaws of a striper do not appear capable of such selectivity—of mouthing the head or the tail of a streamer—today my fly box contains those three patterns tied on 6X long- and short-shank hooks. The streamers, of course, are the same length. Only the shank lengths—consequently the bodies—differ.

I like rods no less than 9 feet long, with the so-called English bend—for the sustaining power of its parabolic action, an invaluable asset when pushed all the way to turn a boring striper heading for a mooring line. Their greater arc, reaching clear to the grip, is a relentless force always capable of withstanding the shock of a quick lunge. The longer rod will extend your casts when you stand waist deep in water fringed with tall marsh grass waiting to snatch your back cast.

Because I build most of my tackle, I develop, through trial and error, line guide size and spacing, grips, and actions which suit the occasion. The striper fly rod is subjected to heavy loads when shooting a forward taper line and should be equipped with friction-free guides. I prefer three butt guides on two-piece sticks, the first having a diameter of ½ inch, the second and third ⅜; and ten snake guides on the top section, of ¼-inch diameter, spaced progressively closer so the probability of line-looping during the cast is all but eliminated. Stainless steel snake guides are essential.

As the logical companion to the oversize butt guides, the grip should be longer—9 inches being ideal. The longer grip allows for lengthening the distance between the hand and the rod butt bearing against the forearm when you are holding steadily against a boring bass.

Fly-Rodding for Stripers

to cast and play the fish without changing hands. Your casting hand becomes conditioned to the feel of the rod's action and responds better to the surge of a strike than does your left hand, normally accustomed to the feel of a few loops of line. Stripers' jaws are cartilaginous, requiring solid, penetrating strikes. Changing hands as soon as the bass is presumed hooked may result in just another fish story.

As to hooks, volumes have been and will be written. Hooks are a matter of preference, a sure cause for argument. Yet, all hooks, regardless of label, are not good striper hooks. Look for these qualities in a 1/0 striper hook: round, slightly offset bend; 2X stout, round wire (not flat-forged); long, slightly turned-in point; well-closed eye; high hardness without brittleness, especially in the point; ability to withstand honing to a *sharp* point; corrosion resistance—stainless steel or tinned carbon steel.

I believe that reflection and opacity are the principal determinants of the effectiveness of a striper streamer. For this reason, mixtures of translucent and opaque materials may be more important than colors. History proves that white, yellow, and blue are basic, provided the materials so colored are built into the streamer with some forethought. White over blue over white, white over yellow over white, and white with barred black and white are sufficient for interesting a striper. Refinements such as shaped, lacquered heads, junglecock or painted eyes lend eye appeal for the angler and, perhaps the fish.

Fly-rodding at night for stripers is an esthetic experience. The bigness of the water, the distant night sounds, the gentle mutterings of the ducks feeding at the river's edge, the sight of the silent muskrat gliding about his nightly business, these set such angling apart.

There is time for thinking private thoughts while you watch the tide begin its return to the sea; time for forgetting the perpetual profit-and-loss sheet and the bank balance. Later, after you have taken your place, waist deep, and feel the pull of the current, you hear the sounds of the bass below you and beyond casting distance. They are on their way.

You try a cast to get the feel and revel at the soft swish of the line coursing through the guides and the *splat* of the streamer dropping at the tail of an eddy. Then you hear the unmistakable *chug* of a rising bass within casting distance. You watch the wake, retrieve to false cast, wait for the next boil.

There it is. *Whop!* You quickly lengthen your cast and send the streamer to twinkle an oar-length ahead of the widening rings.

Whop! He took. There he goes. He's on. You strike hard ... and again. And you smile as the rod grunts. He's headed right for that damned orange mooring. . . .

Fly-Rodding for Stripers

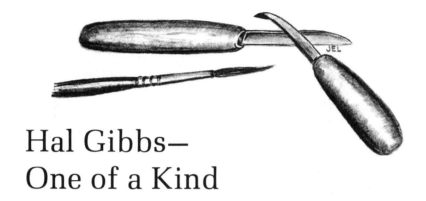

Hal Gibbs—
One of a Kind

On that bleak December day when I knocked on the door of Hal Gibbs' neat, weathered, two-story shingled home, I was excited as a boy. For nearly 20 years I had anticipated meeting the man, a legend wherever serious fly-fishers talked. For Harold Gibbs was to the saltwater flyrod what Theodore Gordon had been to the trout rod.

Business had finally transplanted me in Rhode Island from California, making the visit with Hal Gibbs possible. Despite the many times I had flown from Los Angeles to New York on the "red-eye special," itineraries had not included accounts close enough to Barrington, Rhode Island to make a visit with Hal Gibbs feasible. Now I was standing on his porch within one hour after arriving at the airport.

Years before, when I had been writing a book, I asked Hal for his opinions about taking the striper on the fly. I had caught the hard-fighting linesides on the fly only in the estuaries of Maryland and needed his knowledge about the streamers he tied and used in New England. Hal had been almost as prolix about the striper in his letters as I was later to find him in person for he had studied it for a lifetime and had come to understand its unpredictable nature better than any flyrodder I had heard about or knew.

Waiting, I peered through the trees made naked by winter at Hal's beloved Palmer River, just a surf cast from his door, the river he had mentioned so many times in his correspondence. It had been the proving ground, he had written, for his nearly 50 years of study of the game and shellfish of his native state. And the results, to large extent, were the reason for his becoming Director of Fish and Game for the State of Rhode Island for so many years.

I heard quick footsteps. The door opened briskly. There he stood: little, thin, slightly bent. He eyed me from under the square magnifying glasses he had flipped up under the green shade which was strapped loosely to his head, and said, "Come in, come in. So glad to meet you at last." He held the door open. "Just don't mind the house ... it's messy. I'm whittlin' birds." With this he removed his headgear and preceded me through the kitchen and toward the dining room where he did his "whittlin'."

Knee boots scissored from an old pair of waders stood inside the kitchen door. A flybox, open to the sun, lay on a window sill. A long-billed fishing cap hung from a

Hal Gibbs—One of a Kind

doorknob. Fish and bird prints, some faded, were every-where. The shelves of his book cases were packed with what Hal called his "fishing papers"—the works of fishing writers.

Hal stepped over to the oval dining room table and, from among the little mounds of cedar culls, picked up a miniature bird. He held it in his palm for me to take. It was a cock grouse, magnificent in every detail, including the bristling ruff. "I was just finishing coloring it when you knocked," he said. I felt his eyes studying me from head to toe while I took a long time to examine the artistry of the sculptured grouse. I knew that here was a man who either liked you from the beginning or never would. It is strange that most of the hunters and fishers I have known were —or are—that way. It may be the manifestation of piety, but I have always preferred to believe that it is the matter of caring about sharing one's woods and waters. In the classical sense, I suppose that is piety.

"They're not easy to do . . . the color, that is," he said. "I expect nearly anybody can whittle a bird." Then he smiled. "But the coloring, well, that is something else."

It was then that I noticed that his hands were gnarled from many years of arthritis, and I marveled that they were capable of executing with the keen scalpels and gouges of his art the delicate, yet distinct, feathering needed to produce the so-lifelike miniatures of the upland and water birds he loved so much and of tying the perfect, tiny dry flies for which he was so celebrated. Yet, despite his nearly 80 years, there was a crispness about the man, a lingering youthfulness, conferred by his many years in the outdoors that radiated the satisfaction of having lived as he chose with the enviable reward of total achievement. But, for all his placid charm, Hal was as restless as the rivers he fished.

"It's about time for my sherry," he said. "I'll pour you a glass." While he went to the kitchen, I scanned the titles of the volumes in his book case. Many I would have given much to own. There were first editions, some uncuts, a few leather bound; old tomes enriched with age and irreplaceable pieces of the collector.

When he returned with the sherry, Hal said, "Let's sit down awhile and talk about stripers. That's what you are here for, and it's the nearest thing to fishing for them. Besides, it'll take the rest of the day. I've been whittlin' too much this week anyhow." He pushed a load of tobacco into his crook-stem pipe, lighted it and settled back into his big, overstuffed chair, becoming all but lost in it.

"Necessity is often the mother of invention," he began. "Some of the finest flyfishing in the world was right under my nose—right out there. . ." And he pointed over his shoulder to the Palmer River. "But it took the gas rationing of World War II to make me realize it. Getting to the salmon rivers of New Brunswick and the other places in Canada I fished was just about impossible.

"So I turned to the stripers here at home. With the flyrod, that is. I figured that if they would take spinners and a clam worm, they would take a fly fished in the right spots. We had good runs in those years and we always caught good fish, five to 20 pounds. Like in 1943. According to my records, I took over 300 before late fall that one

season—on the fly, of course. And it proved to be the nearest approach to salmon fishing I know about. Except for the flies, there really isn't much difference. For the striper is a strong, hard-fighting fish and at times just as choosey about taking the fly as any salmon."

He puffed hard on his pipe and looked at it, frowning. "But I don't claim to have started it. Flyfishing for saltwater fish—even stripers—is not new, you know. There was Tom Loving from somewhere down Baltimore way back in the 20's and 30's. He was the first, far as I know, to do much with the stripers in the tidal rivers of the Chesapeake. He and another fellow by the name of Bonbright who flyfished for tarpon years ago really set the pace. And they agreed on one thing, color: red and white.

"I remember that color combination was pretty well proved up in Maine, too. Some years back the old Bangor Pool still had good runs of Atlantic salmon. And when the salmon would not take, some chaps tied on thick red and white bucktails and took stripers, and once in a while a salmon. I believe it was Dana Chapman of Boston who had a lot to do with the development of that color combination up there.

"So the fly game for striped bass is not exactly new or anything that I can lay claim to or take credit for." He grinned then. "But I did invent the Gibbs Striper. It's a good pattern, and it takes stripers if anything will, but don't overlook Theodore Gordon's Bumble Puppy. That was a good streamer and it took many kinds of fish besides stripers! But I believe they were mostly freshwater fish, pickerel, bass and the like."

Hal Gibbs—One of a Kind

Hal puffed a few more times with no result then re-lighted his pipe. "Theodore Gordon's papers were not published until several years after I began flyfishing for stripers. I never met the man. Wish I had. He was a fine gentleman, I understand. He's referred to as the American Halford, you know. I don't know of any higher tribute than that.

"Damn this pipe," he blurted. "Got the thing with to-bacco coupons—sent away for it. It won't smoke and it smells like a burnt waffle." Hal got a straight-stem from his pipe rack then went to the cabinet beside his writing desk to remove his many fly boxes.

"What I look for in a streamer or a bucktail and what I try to show in my own ties is forethought. Too much stuff is wrapped on a hook and called a fly. Color probably means the least, but the size, the shape and the propor-tions mean the most. For if the stripers are on the move, they'll take a plain, well-shaped white streamer as quickly as anything else. Trimmings mean a lot to the fisherman —and to the price tag—and who can tell, maybe sometimes to the fish. I often doubt it."

Hal held up several streamers he had pulled from the sheep's wool of one leather flybook. "Ever look at a hook under a magnifying glass? Try it sometime and be ready for a shock. It looks about as sharp as your big toe. A striper's mouth is hard—lots of cartilage—and a blunt hook may skip from the point of contact right out of its mouth. Besides, your flyrod can put only so much force at the hook point, so the point must penetrate no matter where it strikes."

Hal pushed the point of a Gibbs Striper into his thumbnail. It remained in position and upright. "Like that," he said. "Hooks are more critical in the fly game than too many fishermen think. At first I started with long-shank hooks because they are characteristic of the typical salmon streamer. But it didn't take me long to realize that the short, round-bend hook is better. Stripers strike the head of a baitfish and its the same with the streamer. And that's where you want the hook point. But keep it sharp!"

Hal had been correct about taking the rest of the day to talk about stripers. His knowledge was so vast that each comment mushroomed into a subject of its own, frequently expressed in compelling metaphor, like why a striper will take an artificial twitched through a school of bait fish different in size and color. "I've always believed because to the fish it's a stray, a straggler, about to die. To kill off the weak is nature's way." He paused. "It's the same with humans," he said thoughtfully. "Only the strong succeed, as the saying goes. The weak, the old, perish." And he looked at his gnarled hands. "We all can lift the cup only so many times," he said. "So take it while you can..."

Too soon the afternoon had become evening. And we had conversed about so many topics in addition to stripers: Hal's recollections about Anticosti Island, Cape Breton and New Brunswick, about Alaska and the general salmon situation, the Russian trawlers, the certain depletion of the shellfish off New England. The man was magnificently informed and well educated, but, as Hal said it, relatively little schooled by university standards.

Hal Gibbs—One of a Kind

Probably one of the very few lacking formal education ever to attain the level of Director of Fish and Game for any state, Hal Gibbs did exactly that in the state of Rhode Island. For small as he was of stature and despite his lack of university degrees, Hal Gibbs stood singularly tall in the halls of academe. His influence on fish culture and conservation was nationally known; the knowledge he so painstakingly acquired from the hard seat of a rowskiff and from his own little laboratory on the Palmer River was sought alike by federal committees and the fish commissions of many states.

Although I visited him many times after that first day, I fished with Hal only twice before he waded that last time to the other shore reserved for men who love—and give to—the outdoors. The night we cast for stripers I learned that he did not venture far from the position he took at the start. "When the stripers start, you'll hear them," he said. "As a rule they'll travel the same course. Just stand still where you are and cast to the rise. Some will even bump your waders." His words proved so true.

Hal may have sensed that I wanted to write his biography for he offered access to the notebooks he so diligently kept, and he once gave me a photograph in which he was holding an eight-pound striper he had caught with his "Striper" fly. Now, years later, as I read from those private notes he wrote about his 1956 Alaska experiences, I see revealed again the bigness of the nature he loved and that was Hal's own cathedral. In nature he had inherited without pledge of creed what others attempt to contrive. And that was his aegis.

As he once said: "The best psychiatrist's couch is the

sun-warmed moss of a river bank. If only more people would find that out, the definers of the human emotion would have to close shop. For the man who fishes catches much more than just fish. He comes to accept that the weed, the rock, the very nothing resulting from his cast are as much a part of the game as the fish he sometimes hooks."

What a loss that Hal had never written more than his finely-penned notes. For their accuracy is so pleasing to the naturalist, a delight in factual observation, the words at times fairly twinkling. Ever the student, he identified, counted and defined. And he wrote with instant familiarity upon sighting lesser yellow legs, siskins, waxwings and dowitchers; phalaropes, flycatchers—even the fireweed and lupine of the valleys and slopes, yet admitting that some weeds he could not identify were coarse and rank. He did not simply record that he saw birds on the grass or on a pond. Instead, he saw 14 sandpipers on stilted legs scurrying across the shore; a bald eagle perched nobly atop a stunted spruce on the edge of a cliff; two whistling swans with four half-grown cygnets creasing the surface of the lake.

Hal always airmailed his notes to his wife whom he called "Bill." They itemized the hours he fished, the fish he caught, the fly and how he used it, the food he ate and how it was prepared, how much everything cost, how cold it was; but, always most importantly, what he had seen. Like the bear tracks so huge that, by comparison, his own foot prints were "no larger than the marks of my knuckles." Or the caribou and moose he had counted from the

Hal Gibbs—One of a Kind

window of the Grumman "Goose" from which he scribbled his notes and pencil sketched Mt. Iliamna ". . .pink-white in the sunshine," the Chugash Mountains and the myriad glacial peaks along the way.

Even the way he counted the moose he saw in the lower country below the Talkeetna Mountains reveals the orderliness of his mind. For he did not write that he saw at least 50 moose. He marked each sighting with a pencil stroke and with a diagonal, grouped the count into five's. "See a moose," he wrote. "Another . . . another one." Then the hatch marks totaling thirty-nine.

His hurried writing goes on, ". . .then into the air we go, up, up, almost clawing our way between the mountains. Raw, naked rock, snow fields, miles across . . . crevasses in the glaciers and from the air they are rivers of ice. We have followed one river of ice to the brink of the mountains to slide down over the crest. Suddenly, thousands of feet below is the Pacific Ocean so intensely blue and dramatic. . ."

To Hal Gibbs the outdoors meant more than a bucolic retreat. It was the kaleidoscope of creation in which he perceived himself a miniscule part, but a part none the less. For it all, he was a very private person. He had fixed opinions which he expressed modestly. I remember his saying that he would never be seen twice with a man he did not like, and he never asked for quarter but, if deserving, would give it. But when the subject of conservation arose Hal, the little man, irately grew to twice his size. "People," he said, "no longer care . . . most of them, that is. And those who do have not the power or the political strength to do anything about it. A man who wants to teach his boy how to fish—and catch a few in the process—doesn't pull much weight against wealthy industry that 'just can't afford' to stop its pollution. And if the Federal Government steps in, you'll probably end up with the Corps of Engineers or some such. I've battled that crowd for years, officially and privately, and I found out at the outset that they didn't know as much about ecology (we used to call it conservation) as a woodpecker does about algebra."

Hal Gibbs has left far more than the vestige of a man who once lived. What he did leave will never be lost in the marl of time. For the idyll of his mind is clearly limned in his philosophies, his fishing skills, his "bird whittlin' " so beautifully done with his crooked hands, his knowledge of the rivers and woods of our land he so dearly loved and wanted to preserve and the fish and game therein.

Big, big, little man! As he said, we all can lift the cup only so many times. Today, from my writing desk, I lift the cup to him.

Would that I could have known him long before the winter of his time.

Hal Gibbs—One of a Kind

You Can Bet
on a Full House

A pair and three of a kind have changed the fortunes of man for centuries. And a pair of spinners and one of three patterns of flies—one of the oldest of lures—have changed my angling fortunes for decades. For nearly every fish I have found, fresh or saltwater, that can be termed a "flyrod" fish, and even some that cannot, will take a "full house" in one form or another.

One naturally acquires strong preferences for a certain lure, a pattern or type of fly. He may use it consistently, purely from habit. It may suit his rod and line and cast well. It may fish deeper or shallower than others and be pleasing for it. Or, most importantly, the lure simply may catch fish when others—no matter how highly touted—will not. I look back on the nearly 50 years I have pumped a flyline over the fish of North America and conclude unreservedly that the "full house," except for dryflies, wetflies and nymphs for trout during *selective* feedings, has brought more and bigger fish to the net than any lure I have made, bought or used. And that's a lot of lures! From Maine to Mexico, from California to Florida, it has worked its magic on almost everything with fins that will strike a fishing lure.

The "full house" is a lure for *hunting* fish in strange waters and is a sort of wizard of odds for raising them in familiar waters. It is versatile, fishes like a nymph upstream, minnows its way across, up or downstream, surface fusses like a noisy mini-plug if the rod is held high and, worked at a very slow pace downstream, explores the rocks and ledges like a fingerling rooting for forage.

It is the lure that broadens flyrodding into a near totality. What with the dry and wetflies, the streamer, nymph, surface bug and natural baits (and some flyrodders use them) the "full house" completes the spectrum of fly lures. Countless are the times I have known it to account for smallmouth bass when the most reliable hellgrammite and crawdad had been passed without so much as a touch. And I have seen it work miracles in heavy water on rainbow trout that had not stirred for the very best in the flybook.

It is not partial to genera. Trout, walleyes, pickerel, largemouth, northerns, panfish, stripers, weakfish, bonito, barracudda, bluefish; even the uglies, the catfish and sea robin, find its wobble, spin, streak, undulation and flash to their liking. The only limitation is the leader tip. Northern Pike, muskies, and particularly barracudda and bluefish, the really toothy ones, will bite through or tear monofilament, unless it is so gross that it is impractical for flyrodding. Light wire is necessary then, but it may spook barracudda and blues at times and one simply takes the chance of losing good fish on monofilament or of not getting strikes with the switch to wire—if and when wire will spook them. For "blues" and "barries" can be as cagey as a brown trout with a long memory.

That old discussion about whether a fish strikes the lure for the motion and flash of the spinners or for the weaving, flowing motion of the streamer is probably endless and may never be decided. There are some who say that the spinners really add nothing, that the fish would have taken the streamer for itself. I have strong doubts about that! The spinner adds activity and length to the streamer and is not auxiliary to it. The two, the streamer and the spinner therefore become integral; sound reason for blending the finish of the spinner with the general hues of the streamer. This may seem aesthetic but it is no more so than attempting to arrange the saddle hackles, topping and tinsel body of a fly to represent a dace, smelt or herring. A size 0 double spinner coupled to a ringeye size eight long-shank streamer measures 3⅝ inches overall, ideal for simulating the minnows one would choose if he were a live-baiter. My private hunch is that the copper spinner—Cahill combination which has proved so dependable for brown trout and smallmouth bass, is accepted for the great stonefly which measures about the same length—3⅝ inches.

The small size 0 and one double spinners in the Indiana shape are ideal for flyrodding. Their wind resistance during casting is minimal and their water drag is not objectionable. Even when cast with a fairly light rod and knotted to leader points as small as 2X, the little spinner and fly lure will not overload the rod or require special attention, for the gauge of the blade is thin for easy revolving—preferably wobbling at slow retrieve—and is as comfortable to cast as a number four salmon fly.

Nickel, gold (or brass) and copper finishes are standards and have been for years. Each has a purpose because the clarity of the water, the hue of the streamer, the brightness of the day should be considered. In clear waters the nickel finish is sometimes too flashy and may frighten or at least dissuade the fish from striking. Gold is also flashy but is effective when nickel is not. Copper, which dulls quite rapidly from use, assumes the patina of an ancestral skillet and produces exceptional results for its dulling. For the brown trout one seldom sees and for smallmouth bass, it is my first choice when coupled to a long-shank cahill size eight or ten. The dulled copper, the woodduck and the brown-gray of the·streamer have brought good fish to the landing net that, to this day, I believe I otherwise would never have known about.

This was borne out conclusively on the Susquehanna at Milan. Nylon was in its second season and one could wade the fringes of the river at Vossburg, Milan, Wyalusing and Laceyville without standing in line for a casting position. In those years I fished with Al Beeson and Pete Young. Pete was an advocate of the "clipper" (hellgrammite) fished with the flyrod for bass. Al was a proponent of the ¼-ounce plug which he cast beautifully. I was a nut for streamers but occasionally floated a busy number eight dryfly over the purls trailing the slightly sub-surface rocks and ledges blunting the current.

You Can Bet on a Full House

Al and Pete had traipsed a good distance upriver to gain access to the penninsula which fingered its way for about 200 yards to its tip, flanking a deep backwater, and ending opposite of where I had taken my position. That July day was hot—hot enough to curl the hackle on a dryfly. We were wet wading, the only comfortable way; waders would have been intolerable.

At that time I was struggling in the fly and rod business and had received several dozen size 0 and one sample fly-size spinners in gold, nickel and copper finish, some with hammered surfaces the facets of which were truly scintillating examples of the spinner-maker's art. I had dressed three patterns of miniature streamers—at least they were miniatures for that time—on ringeye number eight, 6X-long hooks: a Cahill, one of the most versatile and productive color combinations I know; a silver-body, teal-wing streamer; and a gold-body, woodduck-wing creation that years later proved its worth for landlocks and squaretails in Maine. Those three patterns and the double spinners became the original "full house" and from that day on the Susquehanna, my first and last choice for fishing anywhere in strange waters.

I have never believed in formula fishing because solid experience disproves it. Yet, the results of that hot July day easily could have made me a one-lure, one-method fisherman. The results spoke for themselves. Always able fishers on any water, Pete and Al were hard to surpasss. With his light-weight, free-spool casting reel and wisp of a rod, Al could flip a tiny runt or crawler out of sight. Pete had a way of roll casting a hellgrammite that would make many salmon anglers envious. But for all their efforts, they netted one fair walleye and two smallmouth. The "full house" accounted for the top creel count that day: six brassy-green smallmouth that, like a brown trout sipping a nymph, had taken the copper spinner-Cahill combination cast upstream on a dead drift. Fished with no more action than what a tight line had given it, the lure fairly dredged the bottom.

Therein lay a profound lesson about the smallmouth. Each had struck the "full house" with the deceiving touch of a canny brown trout, certainly not the mode of feeding for a river smallmouth. At first I was inclined to relate those subtle strikes with the hot weather which, in one sense, satisfied my curiosity. As the season mellowed into fall and eventually took on the chill of late November, however, I learned that the weather had little, if anything, to do with the effectiveness of the "full house" fished on the dead drift. Smallmouth simply are susceptible to the wig-wag (not the spin) of the copper-spinnered Cahill scratching the bottom . And so are brown and rainbow trout!

This was proved time and time again on both the Susquehanna and the Delaware and on their tributaries, notably the Lackawaxen. What better proving grounds are there! From its confluence with the Delaware up to Lake Wallenpaupack, the Lackawaxen had the reputation for generations for being the haven for salmon-size trout. Brawly in places and deep-voiced where shadowed currents, the grinding wheels of time, have carved hollows in its cliffed banks, the Lackawaxen has harbored trout one evaluates in pounds and smallmouth which have extended their outreaches from the Delaware where they were planted about 100 years ago.

A few miles above that point where the Lackawaxen melds with the steady gait of the Delaware, there is an idyllic stretch where an undercut cliff changes the pulse of the current from a boisterous burble to a muttering eddy. One never knows whether a spindle-toothed brown trout or a thumping bronzeback will take the fly. For I have caught both on successive casts in that eddy.

One early June evening I had ventured to that point where wading any further would be disastrous, a fact which I had previously learned. When the flume at the dam is opened, the river is no place to be. I pumped the copper-Cahill into the head of the long pool many feet upstream of the shadows below the cliff. With no action imparted to it except for the current, the little "full house" was swept into the darkness of the long pool.

The expected strike came at the very end of the drift. It was not so much a strike as it was a brief stopping of the course of the lure. The trout, surprisingly a near-black brookie, hesitated uncertainly for a moment then streaked for the sanctuary below the cliff, the surge telegraphing clear to my elbow ... until a barrel knot three sections from the tip failed. The rod flexed upright, lifeless. Then tailing into a long arc, the trout headed downstream, the broken section of leader glinting mockingly in the shadows. Even today I hesitate to guess the length and weight of that brook trout except to say that it had long since attained the length of 20 inches and would have been at home among the Maine squaretails of 30 years ago. For the brief moment it was in the air, it appeared as deep as my hand with the thumb extended.

After I had waded ashore to tie on a fresh leader and another "full house," the same copper-Cahill combination, I was startled by a familiar, soft voice behind me. There stood John Schadt, regional warden, who could appear amorphously like a mist wraith rising from the shadow of a May apple. "I saw the last of that," John said. "That was a real trout." And he explained that such huge brook trout—old breeders—had been released periodically into the Lackawaxen. Then, true to his breed, and despite our friendship of several seasons, John checked my license, we shook hands and he disappeared among the thick brush.

That same picturesque Lackawaxen has yielded many trophy brown trout, two from the same pool. Every trout with the exception of one took the "full house." It was the same in Penn's Creek, at times when a green drake or a Hendrickson would have seemed the logical selection. Sometimes the copper-Cahilll did *not* produce a strike at first but *did* arouse a trout into revealing its residence which I marked for a later effort. Like the 22-inch brown in Fishing Creek which later succumbed to a number eight kapok-bodied light Cahill drifted over his haunt long after midnight one late June night. And the 21-inch brown from the Loyalsock that eventually took the "full house" for keeps after making passes at it for several seasons.

The gold-spinnered, gold-bodied, woodduck-wing pattern has many interesting histories for ferreting out largemouth bass and pickerel from the ponds and lakes,

You Can Bet on a Full House

even the estuaries of the eastern seaboard. From South Carolina to Maine, this version of the "full house" has accounted for fish that had not stirred for the classic spoon, plug or streamer . . . even the plastic worm. Wherever small yellow perch and shiners feed, the gold combination has proved its worth, especially among the shadows of the reeds and tules.

And the larger panfish, the yellow perch and white perch particularly, find the "full house" to their liking. Many are the happy hours I have spent wading the marshes of Maryland's eastern shore and the banks of Massachusetts and Rhode Island casting for the white perch there. They abound in the upper reaches of the little current rivers where the water remains brackish. When the leaves turn russet and gold and the river has taken on the chill of autumn, the white perch mill about in wait for your offering where the tide purls its way to the sea. And occasionally a striper will be there to take the "full house;" but you will be lucky to hold him with your light leader.

Pickerel are partial to the gold and silver versions, and unless you happen to hook one large enough to make everything disappear when it strikes, the spinner shank and streamer will keep the pickerel's teeth a safe distance from the monofilament. This is another advantage to the "full house."

In the late spring of 1973, the landlocked salmon and togue in Maine had been put down by adverse weather and fishing for them was only an exercise. On the hunch that pickerel in the feeder creeks of Big Lake might be active, my wife, Page, and I left Grand Lake to explore that possibility in Little River which snakes its way through a wide expanse of marsh to end in a cove of Big Lake. Following its serpentine course through the reeds, we eventually reached the outfall of the Little River where it broadens into an acre-size pool. Again, the "full house," this time the gold-spinnered woodduck pattern, took five pickerel, none large, the largest a 21-incher which we kept.

With the first gusts of the afternoon wind bending the marsh grass, I cranked up, heading for the sheltered side of the island we had used as a marker (and you had better have several such markers on Big Lake) to troll over the rocky bottom close to shore. With the same rig somewhat riddled by the five pickerel, Page took three smallmouth during the two passes we made. Doubtless had we persisted in our efforts to take the landlocks or togue on streamers, we would have drawn a blank, for only one togue was boated during that week, rather unusual for the productive waters of Grand Lake.

The flyrod has been to sea for many years, but it was not until the last decade or so that it came into its own for the bonito, barracudda, kelp and bull bass of the Pacific. Until recently it was almost pure heresy to deviate from the ten-foot live-bait rod, free-spool reel lined with 20-pound monofilament and an anchovy or a racehorse sardine of which there are no more. But always a bit of the heretic, I found that the "full house" opened the door to many sessions of spectacular flyrodding with the "boneheads," "barries" and bass off the California and Mexican coasts.

You Can Bet on a Full House

Off La Jolla, Oceanside, Ensenada and the unnamed points of the Baja, the little lure performed its magic as it had in freshwater. Invariably the strike, swift and jolting, occured at the depth of three feet or more. What a sight it was to see six-pound bonito streak through the clear, blue water to hit the lure, or to glimpse for a microsecond the arrow-fast dart of a three-foot barracudda as it struck.

If the seas were swelling, a smidgen of wrap-around lead on the spinner shank increased the sink rate for reaching the proper level. And leaders were necessarily of higher test, ten-pound points being entirely adequate. But the barracudda, most vicious and, at times, aerial-minded hellions, required dull-finish, nylon-coated wire traces. Their interlocking, needle-pointed teeth are utterly devastating. I have taken them to eight pounds in the open sea off the Coronados, hardly within sight of those stark islands, on the nickel-spinner, teal-and-silver "full house" which must have had the tincture of anchovy because the barracudda and bonito converged on it in packs. Stripping backing like a 20-pound striper, a "log" barracudda or a racing bonito streaking the surface can make a reel all but smoke and the monofilament fairly whistle through the guides. When they feel the sting of the barb and the power of the rod and shift into overdrive, a "barrie" or a "bonehead" will ask for no quarter.

Hooks for saltwater must be heavier gauge and tin plated at least. Ideally they are made of stainless steel. At that time stainless steel hooks were a few years in the future, but otherwise the hooks for the "full house" were the same long-shank number eight that I had used everywhere. Why the silver-bodied and nickel-spinnered version was more productive than the gold, which I believed better simualted the flash of an anchovy, I do not know. Certainly the barracudda and the bonito do, and I enjoyed their powers of discrimination for it, at least so long as the tackle bag contained sufficient nickel-silver lures to last the day. The life of a sea-going "full house" is short.

Like the bluefish of the East, the barracudda and bonito of the Pacific decimate feathers, tinsel, mylar or hair in short order. And when they are feeding with abandon (What an experience!) they will strike not only the lure but *anything* ahead of it that makes bubbles or streaks. Conversely, when easily spooked, they will shun anything that makes bubbles or streaks ahead of a lure, even the lure, itself. Therefore, snaps and swivels can be a detriment, as was demonstrated on Narragansett Bay during the dog days of August, 1973.

The blues had been schooling sporadically, crazed for the tiny menhaden seeking sanctuary in the upper reaches of the bay. As usual, fishing involved chasing the terns and gulls squawking over the patches of frenzied baitfish herded by the gluttonous but often cagey bluefish. On three successive casts with the nickel "full house," a pack of blues streaked to the lure and exploded around it. At least one blue struck the swivel on every cast, and each snipped the leader like a pair of wirecutters. Gene Beebe, with whom I fish the Narragansett because he is such a natural, a lobsterman by profession and an unusually canny angler to boot, swung his fast boat in pursuit of the next assembly of squealing gulls dipping for the hapless menhaden which were schooled about 300 yards to the south. Enroute I clipped off the swivel from a fresh nylon-coated wire trace and nail knotted the tip of the ten-pound leader to it.

It worked. The first cast had hardly settled before a blue ripped into the "full house" and in ten minutes was gaffed by Gene. Ten chopping, squirming blues came aboard during the next hour, most of them victims of the little "full house" and the nail-knotted wire trace. It is a wrinkle worth remembering.

Although I have used it from coast to coast and have caught my best fish with it, I cannot consider the "full house" a panacea. It is doubtful that any one lure, any single pattern of fly, any one mode or method of fishing ever will be. For just when a fisherman has set aside that one lure, that single pattern of fly, that one way to fish, the great oracle of fishdom will disprove it all. As an example, I recall the time I came upon a still fisherman whose white-top, green-bottom bobber was aligned with the drift of my skiff. As a courtesy, I gently pushed on the inboard oar, to clear his line, as I approached, whereupon he stood up and said, smiling: "Thass all right. You no mind da cork. The waves she bob da fly. An' thass good."

For a few minutes I remained completely confused, until his meaning finally filtered through. He was "bobbing" his fly close to the bottom in a manner most other anglers would not or could not duplicate. And the results of such unorthodoxy? "Any luck?" I asked. Earlier I had released one yellow perch and a smallmouth of marginal size. Each had taken the "full house" twitched along the shoreline. "Just two," he said. But when he pridefully pulled the stringer from the lake edge to show what "just two" meant, I was impressed by the pair of smallmouth of the order of 3 pounds each glistening and twisting on that length of sash cord. Who would guess that any fly dangling from a catfish bobber would interest such smallmouth! But what of a fly that had been rising and dipping near the bottom in pulse with the waves lapping the shore!

The "full house" is legal in most states, illegal in a few but only in certain places at certain times. Some states define "fly" and "fly fishing only" in a manner that excludes weights, spinners and other appended objects which, of course, will outlaw the "full house." So be certain that if you travel to Maine, New Hampshire and some other states that you understand the specific regulations pertaining to the season and the area where you will fish. For example, Maine code defines "Fly" this way: "Fly means a single-pointed hook dressed with feathers, hair, thread, tinsel or any similar material to which no additional weights, hook, spinner, spoon or similar device has been added." However, such definition applies only to areas designated for "fly fishing only." Be sure to familiarize yourself with the regional code.

No, the "full house" is no panacea. But you can always bet on it; for if it serves you as well as it has me—and I must say that I have a feel for it in most waters—you will never be without it, in one of its versions, at least.

You Can Bet on a Full House

The Long and
the Short of It

A good flyrod is a treasure, the melding of the aesthetic with the useful. There is an utter charm in the way it obeys the hand that guides it. As times goes by it will mellow and take on a patina like that of a rare violin enriched with the passing of each season. But just as that instrument needs a good bow to bring forth its latent tones, so does the flyrod need a good line to draw out its power. A class-A rod throughout, regardless of its price tag, will be a miserable thing with a line too heavy or too light. One comparison I can think of is putting a 30-horsepower outboard motor on a tiny skiff or a two-horsepower kicker on a 30-foot cruiser. It just won't work.

Past experience and manufacturers' standards may serve as a rule of thumb for classifying rods. In reality, no strict standards for lengths and weights exist, as I see it. The kind and quality of material in the sticks, the nature of the hardware and the finishing of the rod vary too widely. Compare the actions, length and weight the same, of two high-quality flyrods—one of tonkin cane, one of glass! The proof is in the flexing. One may have a soggy action, the other crisp. And irrespective of impressive equations in rod dynamics, if a rod does not feel good in the hand, all the curves and diagrams wrought of the space age will not change it.

Lines vary in weight and stiffness just as rods do. The unfortunate marriage of incompatible line and rod is a sad situation, indeed. Moreover, most manufacturers are prone to recommend a size lighter line than a given rod will handle well, I suspect to prolong the rod's life. If you accept the rodbuilder's recommendation, however, that at least is a starting point.

What a flyrod is subjected to is amazing. Allowing four casts per minute (believe it or not, in fast runs you will cast more often), the rod will make 240 casts in one hour. Flexing an average of four times per cast, two forward and two backward, the rod will undergo 960 flexures in any given hour. If fishing were to continue all day, at that rate, say from seven in the morning until five in the evening (and that's too early to quit), the casts for the day would total 2400 and the flexures 9600! Allowing for lunch, attending to nature, changing flies, patching a pinhole you finally located in your waders, lining your creel with moss and pine strippings, taking pictures of a fawn and muskrat, wading and just contemplating, deduct two and one-half hours which is more than ample. That still leaves 7200 flexings for one day! As to the number of days you fish in one season, you can extrapolate that count to suit yourself.

A flyrod, then, even when matched with the proper line and placed in the hands of an accomplished angler, is subjected to a pretty rigorous existence.

Weights and lengths all too often are referred to as having some fixed relationship for determining "wetfly" or "dryfly" action. At best, such relationship merely suggests *possible* action; it does not specify it. The lighter the rod, the more flexible, would seem a logical thought. But do not count on it. Some of the recent glass rods of mini-weights and short length have surprising power. I personally do not like them because I favor longer rods which suit my mode of fishing, rods whose flexure I can feel clear through the grip. The bigger rivers have great attraction for me, their long runs, deep holes and complex currents holding secrets which I continuously try to solve. And it takes a big rod to drive the line where it should go.

One such rod is a veteran, three-section, bamboo Phillipson of 9½ feet which I have refinished at least ten times. It is perfect for the big rivers, longer than most rods today but not the least cumbersome. Lined with a DT8F double taper that old friend will place a dryfly as softly as a thistle dropped by an upstream gust. And with a WF8 weight-forward line it will throw a big streamer to kingdom come. I even used it for stripers before I had finished the sinewy glass rod I was building for them. The Phillipson has been a delight ever since I bought it nearly 30 years ago. To attempt to estimate the total weight of the number of fish it has brought to the net is impossible; for it has known the surge of fish from the Atlantic to the Pacific and back again. Brown trout in Penn's Creek, the Lackawaxen, the Beaverkill; salmon in Grand Lake Stream; natives in the Androscoggin; smallmouth in the Susquehanna and the Delaware; largemouth in the Transquaking and Chicamacomico; the bonito and barracudda of the Pacific; stripers and weakfish and blues of the Atlantic. It has taken on all of them with the grace and strength that only a thoroughbred can. It is still going strong for all its six ounces; robust to some perhaps, but gentle in the hand.

Beside it in the cabinet is a Montague of the same vintage, a detachable-butt salmon dryfly rod that has long proved its worth on about everything that takes the fly—and there are not many fish that won't. Larger girthed in the butt section than the Phillipson, the Montague shows the characteristics of the salmon "dryfly" rod of yesteryear. Originally a nine-footer, it had to be shortened after the big striper in the Barrington in 1969 ran out all of the backing. I had snubbed up in a last effort to turn the brute and the Montague snapped just above the male ferrule on the center section. I reworked the entire rod that winter and substituted straight ferrules for the stepped-down originals, giving the rod a new lease on life which it deserved for it had attained a worthy history, the most memorable bit of which was the 14-pound muskie that wolfed down a six-inch streamer. For a muskellunge, that wasn't a fish to boast about, but it was a lot of fish for a flyrod of even 7 ounces!

Then there is the little 7¼-footer (That's an odd length, isn't it!), all of 40 years old. Being part Heddon, part Horrocks-Ibbotson with the tip likely Kingfisher, it is certainly a hybrid, yet one of seemly virtue. In my early days of building rods and tying flies, I acquired an ever-growing assortment of broken rod sections, principally without ferrules. Ferrule design has come a long way since then. The old step-down design was the nemesis of many good rods, for the bamboo had to be necked down to fit the mating part of the ferrule and in exactly the worst and wrong place—in the joint.

A dollar being a pretty valuable item in those days, I salvaged anything that could serve a useful purpose to the fisherman. And so it came about that the 7¼-footer was born. When completed it had a slender cork grip and reel seat with hand-wrought aluminum sliding ring, an agate stripper, straight German-silver ferrules and black oxidized guides wrapped with light-brown, fine silk. It was a gem, a pure joy on the stream, despite its questionable lineage, but it performed like a thoroughbred, fairly outdoing other rods whose brand names one spoke with reverence. Duplicating that wisp of a rod would be most doubtful, given the same conditions and the materials to choose from. Its one failing was that it spoiled me. It cast an H line, 9- and even 12-foot leaders tapered to 6X and a number 16 Cahill like a gently settling mist.

It is semi-retired now. Perhaps no more than twice a year will I take it from its place for an hour or two of exercise in search of a brace of white perch in the Palmer River. At long last it shows the marks of time. There are traces of black between the strips of bamboo, and I know the little rod's days are numbered. For that I treat it ever so gently the few times I use it each year, but it always will be a keepsake. It has given me many hours I like to remember.

Many glass rods complete my collection. I am developing a keen sense of appreciation for the glass rod; for its strength, its ability to withstand overloading, its light weight. Perhaps its outstanding virtue is reproducibility, which even the best bamboo rods lacked. And for a maverick of sorts, it is certainly building a tradition in its own right. Many of today's anglers never would have become flyrodders had it not been for fiberglass and the rods made from it at prices they could afford.

I flyrod for saltwater fish a large part of each season. There is no question that the trout rod and bass rod are out of place in saltwater; not so much for their ability to cast well enough and hold a fish, as for their corrodible hardware. Line guides must be stainless steel, the ferrules and the reelseat at least corrosion resistant, the grip longer for higher grasping and support under the forearm. So equipped, the glass rod admirably meets the test, taking the punishment from long casts billowing ahead of a streamer large as your finger, surviving the "whack" of the strike when you drive the barb into the hard jaws of a striper, withstanding the marvelously long runs that accelerate, at times, if the fish angles away and "tacks" against the tide.

Taking the flyrod to sea for the first time is an experience that will not be soon forgotten. It's big stuff! You have to think big, act big, expect the big. And if your tackle needs apology, leave it home. That applies to the rod, the reel, the line, the backing, the leader, the flies—the

The Long and the Short of It

complete outfit. To offer a questionable analogy, you just can't drive a spike with a tack hammer!

My first choice is a straw-colored stick of nine feet, two inches having a ten-inch choke grip, ample reel seat, oversize line guides (stainless, of course), three light-weight spinning guides on the butt section, an O-ringed ferrule. It will shoot an 11-weight torpedo head a country mile, after one backcast. The action is on the soft side, according to some standards, but that I like; it compensates for whatever errors I am responsbile for and soaks up the unexpected thrust from a striper. If it has a failing, it is the tendency to be too light at the strike. And for that reason I ram the barb home not once but twice for good measure. For handling the tender-mouthed weakfish, it is superb, following the swift lunges with a tenacity that virtually assures the hook will not tear free.

There are others in the rod case, some samples for testing, others with histories both good and bad. Rods are such fascinating things! One gets to treasure them like fine, old books. We gather them through the course of years, sometimes wondering what to do with them. But, like those old books, they remain in their own very special place, some used only once or twice, others many times. Perhaps each rod is a book in itself. I look at one and the sounds of a river fill my study as clearly as if I read the words from a page with a turned down corner.

Just wriggling a good rod about while armchairing is half the pleasure of it. And perhaps good rods should have names; Betsy, Maggie, Patsy and the like. I haven't got around to that yet. But it's food for thought when I'm in my dotage.

A Fly Is What
You Want It to Be

The literature is filled with millions upon millions of words about flies; their patterns, histories, sizes, when to fish them, how to fish them, how to tie them. Through the years I have contributed a few words on those subjects myself. But I have yet to see anything written about throwing away even one fly.

Most flyrodders accumulate flies with an almost unholy passion. They buy, tie, borrow, trade and even pilfer them, forever filling their fly boxes and leather books with them until the contents look like a squashed hen. But I am not the one to dissuade them! Having a new box of trout or salmon flies is like Christmas every time it is opened, and it forever seems that the patterns in somebody else's fly boxes are more fascinating than one's own.

One of the best days astream I can remember occurred on Fishing Creek many years ago. Another fellow's Hendrickson was responsible for it. I found it dangling on a bit of leader snagged on a spruce twig about rod-tip high. There were at least a dozen Hendricksons just like it in my own fly box, but that one dangling from that twig for one reason or another had most singular appeal. I finally retrieved it after all but climbing the tree and nearly tearing my waders. In those days a good dryfly was worth about 35 cents. Perhaps I liked it because it was like the Hendricksons I tied, the hackle extending a couple of turns further down the body than was traditionally correct. I caught six good trout with it.

Later that afternoon, Al Beeson came wading downstream. When he recognized me he hailed me at once. He was out of Hendricksons, he said, in fact he had lost his last one that morning in a spruce tree that had snatched his backcast. Could I spare, say, half a dozen just like the others I had given him two or three weeks ago. . . I did, of course, but was somewhat abashed that I had not recognized my own handiwork in that fly I spied dangling from that spruce twig!

Whether you know an insect by its scientific (Latin) name or by the name of the artificial supposedly representing it is the matter of circumstance and preference. The former may be more learned to some minds; and perhaps it is, but I do not think the trout is at all offended if we continue to call a March Brown a March Brown. It would be interesting, however, to hear the retort from most anglers to the question: "Have you a spare *Stenon-*

A Fly Is What You Want It to Be

ema vicarium? I just lost the last I had in a good trout a few minutes ago." And what of the plurals? One must be most careful using the proper declension at a time like that! Would the plural be *vicarii* or *vicaria?* Or maybe *vicariums* now that pluralizing has undergone such radical changes in recent years. It used to be that a hippopotamus multiplied by two became hippopotami; now it's hippopotamuses. So maybe *vicariums* might be right after all.

Anyway, the March Brown is a good pattern and has been (in either its British or American form) for hundreds of years. So are the Grey Fox; the Cahills, light and dark; the Quill Gordon; Hendrickson; Adams; Iron Blue Dun; Mallard Quill; Ginger Quill; Green Drake and a whole host of others beautiful as all get out, ad infinitum. . .

Where does that leave the newcomer to the stream, that diligent chap who has devoured all the literature that he could lay his hands on describing what flies to use where? Exactly nowhere. For if he purchased (he'll tie later) just two of each mayfly pattern in each of the sizes that approximate the natural in its nymphal, dun and spinner stages, he would have so many flies that he'd need a gillie just to tote them. Add the stoneflies, caddis flies, terrestrials and many of the "specials" all good fly assortments contain and he would have to hire another gillie to bear the load.

Is there a solution? I'm still trying to arrive at one.

And consider the chap who sits down at his vise to tie some Quill Gordons. Behold! He finds he has no dun hackle, that one item whose hue has been the cause for heated argument for so many years. He roots through his choice capes and saddles, even the little plastic envelopes containing the odds and ends he so patiently saved. But not a single dun hackle worth a look is there. Breaking tradition, he substitutes grizzly for the dun, ending up with a pretty formidable looking fly. And he ties six of them and goes fishing.

The Quill Gordon, or should I say *Epeorus pleuralis* (Or is it *Iron fraudator* where you live?), is hatching beautifully, the trout are rising for it and the day holds promise. The grizzly-hacked Quill Gordon makes its first drift to disappear quickly in the ring made by a rising trout. And it happens five, six, a dozen times. That fellow is beside himself with the realization that he has created a fly that raises trout as well as Theodore Gordon's masterful prototypes. But the hitch here is that only Gordon, himself, knew the hue of the dun hackle he used to fashion his wonderful fly. Chickens being what they are, there is sound reason to believe that the duplication of that hackle had been most remote for years. Does that mean that now there are *two* Quill Gordons!! Of course! And there are probably at least 59 others just as effective. Heresy? I do not mean it to be.

So the inventor of the "new" Quill Gordon becomes so enraptured with his findings, that he proceeds to give the fly a name. "Let's see," he muses. "It was a Quill Gordon but had a grizzly hackle—not the dark barred, but that light-barred chinchilla. And the quill body didn't have a fine gold wire rib because I was out of that, too. So what shall I call it?"

A Fly Is What You Want It to Be

Now that chap's name was, say, Archibald Hinkle. Archie sat up most of the night, after he had put his trout in the freezer, trying to conjure a name for his new so-Gordon-like creation. Being human, he naturally wanted his name attached to the name of that fly in some respect. So he struggled with all sorts of combinations of words, even wrote down a table of particulars about the fly and the experiences of that day:

> Name: Archibald Hinkle
> Variations: Chinchilla hackle instead of dun;
>   no gold wire rib on quill body
> Original: Quill Gordon
> River fished: Little Spruce
> Results: six brown trout that were rising
>   to Quill Gordons
> Day: May 10th.

Putting all the facts together posed a problem and Archie tried all sorts of clever mixtures of words. Even acronyms didn't work. His first candidate was Archie's Little Spruce Gordon; his second, Hinkle's chinchilla-hackle Quill Gordon. But then he wanted a word like variant in there somewhere but decided against it because the hackles were not long enough for a variant (according to strict standards, of course). It just didn't fit. Archie continued in his efforts to hit upon a suitable name.

Finally it came to him that he had created a "special" fly, not a mere variation. It had special powers for luring trout! So scratching his earlier efforts, Archie called it very simply, "Archie's Special Spruce" fly; the unrecognized acronym notwithstanding, and it had entered in the catalogs of the great, another "special" to swell the ranks of the already bulging American fly lexicons.

The new fly continued to take trout, its disguise as a Quill Gordon prevailing each season, until other anglers, perhaps some out of chinchilla hackle, created new versions of the Special Spruce Fly. Still everybody caught trout, the trout none the wiser, and there was great happiness among the clan.

Bless Archie's soul and bless all the others'. For that's how flies are come by. And isn't that what it's all about!

This little fable is more factual than mythical, but it may serve to illustrate one significant point. Not only does the Quill Gordon take trout when they are rising for the *Epeorus pleuralis* (or *Iron fraudator*) but so does "Archie's Special Spruce" fly and the Lord, alone, knows how many more. The conceptions of man have been legion in his efforts to simulate that bug!

Will he ever get the *perfect* imitation? Is it really necessary that he achieve that goal? If only those anglers fishing the Quill Gordon on any given stream caught trout during the hatches of the natural *epeorus*, perhaps near simulation would be imperative. But that is not the case. Far too many creels have been and will continue to be heavy with trout that accepted flies not resembling the natural at all.

An able flyrodder equipped with but one good fly, and who knows how and where to place it will have trout at the end of the day when another fellow, not knowing the where and the how and the secrets of the river, but forever

A Fly Is What You Want It to Be

changing flies all day, will have little if anything to show for his efforts.

There is nothing sacred about the tie of a fly. Don't misunderstand me. I have the deepest respect for the names of Hewitt, Bergman, Gordon, Steenrod, Cross, Hendrickson, Jennings, La Branche, Leisenring, Schwiebert, Wetzel, Dette, Darbee, Martinez, Wulff, Flick, Marinaro, Atherton, Blades, Stevens, Donnelly, Harger, Pray, Rhode, Gresh, Cartile, Aucoin, Loving, Fox, Gibbs, and the hundreds of others of the American anglers who have contributed so thoroughly to the selection and mixtures of hackle, quill, fur, floss and feathers. Without them, fly tying and flyfishing as we know it today, would be far less definitive than it is. But, it has a long, long way to go. How much they gained from the pioneering of Berners, Barker, Denny, Venable, Walton, Cotton; and later Ronalds, Hofland, Pulman, Pritt, Halford and the host of other British greats, is self-evident. A twist here, a special treatment there, a slightly different hook, and a new fly is born, another soldier among the ranks that march across the pool to the rhythm of the flyrod.

So we continue to be the experimenters in pursuit of the perfect fly, yet untied. For soon as one is heralded as such, another Archie Hinkle will appear on the scene to muss up the archives and set off a whole new trend to profit the feather merchants and hackle benders of America. And why not!

Take it from there. You can go fishing with a handbook and a folding magnifying glass, forever trying to duplicate a nymph, a dun or a spinner, or you can learn to match the *size* of an insect with a reasonably good representation of its hue and type and take trout with it. I never yet saw a trout—or any other fish—equipped with a micrometer and color spectrum. Whichever choice you make, the fun is in the doing. And some of my dearest friends still ponder which is the better way to go.

A fly is what you want it to be. Regardless of how you get it there or how you get it back, hopefully with a fish fastened to it, *where* you put it, and how, are the biggest secrets of all. As Nev Learn managed to drum into my head: "Cast where you're lookin'. The fly will take care of itself. Just be sure you look at the right spot."

The fly *is* what you want it to be. It is the only hook in the entire process. Sooner or later you will get the point.

A Fly Is What You Want It to Be

"Salty" Bass of
the Eastern Shore

From the foot of the old wooden bridge where we slipped the skiff through the marsh grass and into the river, the slow-moving water bending into the darkness of the thick woods was a welcome sight. Mixed with the marshy scent of the brackish river, the odors of spring were everywhere. Even the usually censorious clack of the grackles seemed pleasant. It was May; salty bass time.

Several years had passed since our last excursion into these upper reaches of the river; yet the scene had not appreciably changed. Except for a few more dead pines and gums having succumbed to the seasonal northeasters, to sprawl askew beside those of earlier seasons, time may have stood still.

We were drifting on the tide of one of the rivers of the eastern shore, one of the winding systems that drains the marshland of the Chesapeake. Quiet and canal like, it has little flow but for the in-and-out movement of the tide which makes the upper reaches a natural haven for the growth of an almost impenetrable tapestry of lilies and snags laced with vines and patched with the imperishable tuckahoe.

The next hairpin turn was less than 100 yards downstream. What lay beyond was always a fascination, because an eastern-shore tidal river may wind 20 times the straight-line distance from its rise to the estuary where it becomes lost in the bay. So serpentine are these rivers that the span from one reach to the next may be a mere hundred yards yet, by water, a mile or more around.

I had been busy tying a needle knot and was not aware of what Page was doing except that she was casting, from the slight movement of the skiff. Suddenly, in that rising voice women resort to when they are in doubt about anything, she said: "I'll never boat it, if it gets into those roots." I looked up from my knot tying at the warp of her rod and knew she was fast to a thumper. Like all "salties" the bass churned the water into a tawny suds then headed downstream toward that cluster of roots, the line creasing the surface of the lazy river, the reel buzzing like a summer locust.

I pushed on the right oar to better her position just as the rod straightened. Page lifted the rod and stripped in line. The bass splattered the surface with a series of thumps, then bored for the opposite side of the river.

"Salty" Bass of the Eastern Shore

My wife has the penchant for doing things well, and she was proving it again. My advices were needless, although I am sure I must have told her the usual—"keep the pressure on . . . hold your rod high"—the things husbands always say when their wives are hooked into a fish.

When it was within reach, I grasped the bass by the jaw and heaved it aboard. "That's the biggest bass you've ever caught," I said.

"You're a good gillie," she replied.

The river we were drifting whorls and wriggles its way from the trickling spillway of an old mill pond all the way to that indefinite flat where the river melds with the waters of a lesser bay, an estuary of the Chesapeake. It is strongly brackish, like the others of the marshland yet has abounded in largemouth bass that have thrived in the environment.

Opinions differ about the origin of these bass. Some say that they have always been there, at least 100 years, according to some records. Others say that the bass, planted years ago in the ponds formed by damming the river headwaters, were washed into the tidal rivers or had access to them when the old hand-structured dams let go, incident to the hurricanes which still sweep through the marshes.

Whether the bass had always been there naturally or had been transplanted by man or a twist of nature is moot. I do know that the dam at the headwaters of this river has failed and been rebuilt at least four times in the past 50 years, and this may account for the presence of the largemouth in the river.

Regardless of their origin, these "salty" bass are more dogged, more ornery than largemouth I have tackled elsewhere. And I have fished for them in many places, from southern California to Maine. Stirring up a boil big as a washtub from the moment they feel the muscle of the rod, they are pure hell raisers. And they are different from other largemouths in two respects.

Instead of responding to the hour of the day to feed, as do most freshwater fish, they feed on the rising tide or at the beginning of the ebb, quite like a striper or a weakfish. High noon on a breaking tide may be the peak hour; evening, at low ebb, a waste of time. The old rule of fishing at daylight and at sundown does not hold true here; unless, of course, the tide is right. The second difference is that while they feed on the fauna most largemouth do, these bass prey, in addition, on fauna generally believed the staple diet of saltwater fish.

Leaving their potholes and the channel depths at high tide, they will cruise through the narrow guts, just flushed to feeding depths by the bay tide, to engulf not only the usual bull minnow or frog one might expect but a small blue crab scuttling in retreat, perhaps a small eel. The salties can be spotted then by the tell-tale of their dorsals weaving through the rope-like roots that fringe the banks.

I first knew of the salty bass of Maryland's eastern shore some 30 years ago. After studying topographic maps for hours, I scouted the waters accessible by road and soon learned that exploration was limited to viewing the rivers from the old plank bridges which appeared without warning from the hummocks of head-high grass. But the dark, quiet waters that flowed under those two by twelve planks surely contained bass, I thought.

Inquiry in two nearby villages, deep in Sunday torpor, was not very fruitful. Discouragingly, the natives who would even talk about it all, had little, if any, regard for the freshwater "ba-yus", some even going so far as to call it a trash fish. But this was understandable. "Rock" or striped bass of the bay waters were the only fish held in esteem. They, and the hardheads, their idiom for the croaker, were the only fish the natives ate, despite the other fish available to them for the taking.

The next day, however, I found two old timers who were exceptional for I found they fished for the salty bass. They were anachronous for not being livebaiters and preferred instead to fish with "foolers"—their name for the silver-scaled, shallow diving plugs they swore by.

I met these two gentlemen purely by accident in Sam Jones' store—that emporium on the shore long known locally for its total dishevelment yet considered the source for nearly one of anything anyone wanted to buy and for which it became nationally famous a few years ago. Its disarray was almost classic. Sam mysteriously could find a slab of bacon hidden between a pair of age-checkered rubber boots and an umbrella or a box of ladies drawers sandwiched between a bag of hogfeed and assorted copies of his latest treatise on religion, at ten cents per copy—the books, that is, autographed, if you liked.

Elmer and his uncle, the two old timers, were there buying chicken feed as I recall. They must have overheard my question to Sam about the bass. Sam dropped his

"Salty" Bass of the Eastern Shore

glasses which swung from a shoestring and asked: "Ba-yus? You must mean rock. Ketch them in the bay." Elmer emerged from behind a column of sundries.

"He's talkin' about tuckeyhoes," he said. So we talked. "If'n it's ba-yus—tuckeyhoes—maybe I kin hep ya," he said. And after listening to Elmer and his uncle, who soon joined into the conversation, I all but invited myself for a float trip down river with them.

Years of fishing for bass had conditioned me never to be surprised at the tackle or the techniques other bassers use. After hearing how Elmer and his uncle fished, I had to see it done. And when they asked me to try the lower reaches the following morning I was eager. In fact I was waiting for them at the appointed place, one that I had crossed over earlier: a 2-plank bridge near which they kept a skiff hidden in the tall grass.

They peered curiously at my flyrod and trappings, but I feigned ignorance in the art of bassing, the better to lean on their willingness to show me how to "ketch a tuck-eyhoe." So I stated that I would watch them, at least for awhile.

Their style *was* unorthodox, at least to me. To many would have seemed ludicrous. Yet, primitive as it was, it exactly suited the environs—and the bass—as Elmer quickly proved.

They skittered their "foolers" from cane poles about 11-feet long, and how they handled that gear! With a mere flip, like opening a hinge, they dropped their "foolers" into a space the size of your hat. Elmer was especially proficient at this reel-less game. Rolling the cane pole between the palm of his hands, he would shorten or lengthen the line in a wink, by winding it between the tip and the first node, where the line was tied. Then, dangling the "fooler" he would drop it into a small opening among the lily pads or roots, to lead it in circles or bob it up and down until a salty struck. I have never since witnessed a technique equaling Elmer's antics with his cane pole for controlling the placement and action of a plug.

And Elmer caught bass. Thumpers! Five of them! When a bass smashed the plug, the game became the matter of muscle and fin power. Elmer would haul back and the bass would splatter like a tilted outboard at full throttle, slithering through the network of snags, pads, vines and tuckahoe. Elmer usually won. But, once as I watched, he did not. For the salty is capable of putting on a surprising performance, even when horsed with a cane pole—like that one of surely six pounds that broke off the tip clear to the first joint, to disappear hell-for-leather downstream, the six-inch tip of the splintered pole trailing like a crappie bobber.

Flycasting, as Elmer and his uncle saw it, was utter foolishness. They had read about it in the magazines but reckoned that the salty would not be much interested in "them gee-gaws" of feathers and hair wrapped around a hook, but they gave me the opportunity of trying it. They even offered to boat their cane poles and paddle the skiff to those places I would point out. In two hours the tide would be low, they said, and the bass would hole up until the first tide, early the following morning. That gave me about an hour.

"Salty" Bass of the Eastern Shore

As the skiff drifted toward a sandy bar, I flipped the double spinner and streamer to the near side of a cluster of roots, a likely looking place for a salty. The "full house" twitched only twice before the strike. Prepared for another salty at least the size of one of the five on the sash cord tied to the oarlock, I struck accordingly, waiting for the expected surge. A white perch, large for his kind but hardly what I expected, came aboard after a creditable struggle. This was no way, indeed, to vindicate the flyrod, especially before Elmer and his uncle. They remained courteously quiet, however, even after I had caught eight more perch. All were carbon copies of the first and were caught on eight successive casts.

In time the tide sneaked us around a sharp bend and under overhanging cedars, their shadows painting the water dark as tar. Here the lily pads were all but gone and the river widened. A water-soaked limb, caught in a web of roots and nodding slowly below the far bank, coaxed the tide into a quiet eddy. It was a simple back-hand cast away.

The spinners landed with a soft spat, twinkled briefly, then disappeared. A jolt, definitely not a snag and certainly not a white perch, arched the rod sharply. I struck hard, then again, and I knew it was a salty *and* that it was solidly hooked. As expected, the salty thumped and circled in a space no wider than the sweep of a yardstick, then headed for the shelter of the roots and the nodding limb. Twice the bass demanded line, bulling against everything the rod had. Then it stopped and eased to the surface, head upright, jaws opening and closing slowly. I could see the spinners dangling but the streamer was out of sight.

"Watch out" Elmer's uncle yelled, "that one's big enough to tow the skiff." As if it had heard, the bass headed downstream to do exactly that, and for the first time my companions did a lot of talking.

After I had lifted the bass aboard, Elmer's uncle said: "Better'n six pounds . . . mebbe close to seven." And he was right. That night on meat scales, my first salty bass balanced six pounds, eleven ounces. A good bass then, a better bass now, and one larger than any of the five on the stringer.

I knew that the flyrod had been somewhat vindicated after Elmer asked: "How much does a rig like that cost, and how long does it take to learn to switch that skinny pole back and forth?"

During the 30 years since that first encounter with the salty largemouth, I have learned to respect the fish for its characteristic of feeding according to the tide rather than the hour of the day. It has been rewarding because that single trait, which persists throughout the entire fishing season, sets the salty apart from his freshwater kin. Yet, I believe that few bass anglers who frequent the tidal rivers are aware of it.

A few years ago, the dependable "full-house"—double spinners and big streamer—accounted for 23 salties and a sore wrist during two days. All but three were released to be caught another time. Those two days had been hot. Still, the fishing was best during the hours generally reserved for a couple of beers and maybe a nap: from two

"Salty" Bass of the Eastern Shore

hours before and for two hours after high noon. The tide had been right, peaking about 11 and 12 and I had stopped fishing, as the action tapered off, about two o'clock each afternoon.

This is not the environment for stunt rods and toy tackle. Leave your trout rods home. Use tackle suited to the task: a rod you can depend on to handle the load of casting a "full-house" and holding against a bass when you must; a good reel spooled with floating level line; a leader strong enough to convey the message when you sink the hook into a bucket-faced bass. A salty could not care less if your monofilament tests 10 or 20 pounds. So use 20. It's a margin of safety, if you have to "straight line" a bass with notions of his own.

When you have struck into one of these fellows in an opening no bigger than your hat, your tackle has to be persuasive. If it isn't, you will spend most of your time fumbling shoulder deep in the dark waters trying to extricate your streamer from a comb of roots, or salvaging a salty that is still on and trying like hell to get off. The single-hook streamer, incidentally, unlike the plug or spoon, is a built-in safeguard against becoming foul hooked when the salty tries to lead your gear and you through the labyrinth of his obstacle course. Once you have experienced the loss of a good fish—bass or otherwise—because a dangling, free hook became buried in a root or stump, you will never forget it. Other reasons for using stout gear are the stripers in the lower reaches that are as long as your arm and the pickerel as long as your left leg that frequent the upper reaches.

Since that first day with Elmer and his uncle, I have caught the salty their way—with the fooler and cane pole—and by casting handcut pork chunk and rind; when livebaiting for pickerel with a fat, five-inch bull minnow below a float five feet up; by thumbing a knuckle buster while tossing a blue-headed, one-ounce plug on night tides. I have caught far more than my share, however, with a flyrod casting from a skiff, and I have taken many by wading—tricky business in these waters. Firm footing is rare because the edges of the river are abundant in thick, false bottoms, the fabric of weeds, rotted vines, leaves and roots, mortared with muck. And because sinking from knee to waist deep is deceivingly slow, the angler may be unaware that he is in for some mighty unpleasant struggles until he tries to move. When safe, however, wading can be effective and offers the opportunity to cast into areas not always approachable by skiff. One caution: wet wade in old pants and sneakers. In the muck, a ripped wader will anchor you like a bridge pillar.

Rowing back toward the old wooden bridge that evening, I realized that Page had caught more salties than I. We seldom kept more than two and there were four on the chain stringer. I remembered catching two which I released. How come!

Page must have read my expression for she just sat there grinning. Well, when you're a good gillie, you haven't much time to fish, I thought. Besides, even when I take on the role of gillie (When don't I?) it's nice to remember that I have a wife who puts up with the hackle fluff she forever tries to catch in the vacuum cleaner, the

"Salty" Bass of the Eastern Shore

damp wading brogues that I didn't dry and left on the kitchen drainboard, and the smelly clam worms in the breezeway that I always forget but have to use at times when the stripers refuse the best of my feathered inventions.

Although we were only moments away from the old wooden bridge, Page already had pulled the hood of her nylon jacket over her head and pushed her hands up into the sleeves. Like the strings in an orchestra tuning up, the mosquitoes had begun to prepare for their sundown concert.

"Bugs and all," Page said, "I hope it never changes. There just aren't many places like it left anymore are there?" "Nope," I said, batting at a mosquito big enough to wear a vest and bow tie that was auguring into the back of my hand. "Not very many."

And it is so. Few fishing areas of the eastern seaboard have remained so nearly pristine as the marshes of the eastern shore. Adequately aided by the ubiquitous mosquito and the indefatigable sheepfly, they seem to have naturally withstood the outreach of burgeoning suburbia. Hopefully the mosquito and the sheepfly will continue to prevail, and with such luck we will be fishing for the salty bass at least once each season for a few more years.

JEL

Season's End

There is the time when the season ends, when we put away our rods for the year with regret, and we think back on the many hours we have waded the rivers we love, hopefully to match our skills with the wild and latent knowledge of the trout, salmon, bass and others we pursue. Sometimes at season's end we emerge the victor, often the loser, but always, always the wiser, because each season bestows its gains and losses in temporal elegance, marking our calendars with the strokes of time.

There is the time at the end of the season when we retreat to prepare for the advent of the next to come, its eventual arrival becoming more precious for our counting the days. And we look to those days when, again, we may wade the river, casting strong and true to a fish that will pluck our fly. It is so long to wait, and each season the waiting grows longer. We sort and resort the flies and leaders that appear from the crannies of a hat band, the lamb wool's patch on our vest, from our pockets and dozens of fly boxes, finding many in the wrong places which were put there in haste while we were changing flies and gear astream. When we find an old frizzed-out Cahill, an almost hackle-less March Brown, perhaps a Quill Gordon whose quill body long since has disappeared, we remember so very clearly the stories that go with each one, solid reasons for their not being retired because they take us back to another time.

There was the time when the sheer joy of casting a fly and taking a trout or two were enough, when the largest trout or bass or salmon alone was not the crass cause for claiming a fantastic prize. It wasn't the size of the catch that mattered so much as knowing that the owl, whom we probably had named, still watched from his own private limb; that the punctual muskrat, making his rounds, still was there; that the sight of a huge stonefly scurrying to safety within the folds of the bark of a windfall meant good fishing in the days to come—if one knew how.

There was the time when fathers and sons solved the secrets of the river together and came to know one another in the way that prevails through their whole lives, each knowing the song of the river for its true meaning; when to reach a mile of fishing water they did not cross river after river reeking with the filth of man's latter day genius just to get there.

There was the time when man was not a number but a name, a name of which he was very proud and he did not fear for losing that number to become without identity; and for his name he was autonomous, morally responsible for his decisions and freely questioning the desideratum that all was well when he knew it was not. Many times he thought out his own solutions while drifting a fly over a brawling run.

There was the time when the conifers and aspen of youth were ever so near. Close and tall, they were the shrouds, the watersheds which kept our streams and rivers, the very aegis of our lives, healthy and full-flowing. In the canopy of their shadows was captured the sweet dampness of dew to be released when the earth grew parched. But when the trees were cut away, monstrous weeds emerged to suck away the strength of the saplings yet remaining, for without the shelter of the trees the weeds became naked and unrestrained.

There was the time when living was not the paradox of destroying only to survive another day.

There came the time when many of us were lost in the dust of where the conifers and aspen once stood, searching for that which we may find again only in recall. Perhaps the remembering will be the reward for just having lived and expiation for unwittingly having been vassal to

Season's End

the feigned intellect of technology forever kindling from the ashes of its last phase unto the next.

But there was a time . . . yes there was. So long ago. So long ago I sometimes wonder when it was. Yet, time never can be turned back. But the nostalgia at season's end, self-justifying as it is, is the essence of time, the very marrow of man's bones.

So go fishing! For there will come the time when casting the fly will be legend, lost in the sounds of machines and the devices of tomorrow. Yet, man needs so much to know again the very existence from which he evolved but cares not enough to pause long enough to seek it. If only he would take a little time. . .

There was a time. There is a time. And the fisherman knows both of them at season's end.